Poetry as Prayer
Saint Francis of Assisi

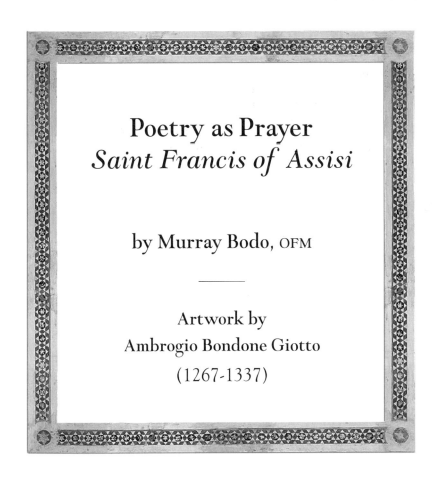

Poetry as Prayer
Saint Francis of Assisi

by Murray Bodo, OFM

Artwork by
Ambrogio Bondone Giotto
(1267-1337)

Pauline
BOOKS & MEDIA
BOSTON

Library of Congress Cataloging-in-Publication Data

Bodo, Murray.

  Poetry as Prayer : Saint Francis of Assisi / Murray Bodo.

        p. cm. — (The poetry as prayers series)

Includes bibliographical references.

  ISBN 0-8198-5940-0 (pbk.)

  1. Francis, of Assisi, Saint, 1182–1226. Cantico di frate sole. 2.
Christian poetry, Italian—History and criticism. 3. Prayer in litera-
ture. 4. Prayer. I. Title. II. Series.

  BV489.F74 B63 2003

  242'.72—dc21

                                2002014153

Printed and published in the U.S.A. by Pauline Books & Media,
50 Saint Paul's Avenue, Boston, MA 02130-3491.

www.pauline.org

Pauline Books & Media is the publishing house of the Daughters of St.
Paul, an international congregation of women religious serving the Church
with the communications media.

1 2 3 4 5 6 7 8 9   11 10 09 08 07 06 05 04 03

*To my Franciscan Brothers of
the Province of
St. John the Baptist*

Contents

Chapter i

Poetry and Prayer

A good poem is the shortest distance between you and the subject.

—*Mark Van Doren*

We make out of the quarrel with others rhetoric, but of the quarrel with ourselves, poetry.

—*William Butler Yeats*

Take a commonplace, clean and polish it, light it so that it produces the same effect of youth and freshness and spontaneity as it did originally, and you have done a poet's job.

—*Jean Cocteau*

Poetry is the opening and closing of a door, leaving those who look through to guess what is seen during a moment.

—Carl Sandburg

For the sake of a single poem, you must see many cities, many people and things, you must understand animals, must feel how birds fly, and know the gesture which small flowers make when they open in the morning.

—Rainer Maria Rilke

The above quotations were collected by Donald M. Murray, one of my first writing mentors. An inveterate collector of apt quotations, he supplied reams of them from writers on their craft, quotations which I'm sure many of us teachers who attended his writing workshop at the University of New Hampshire in the late '60s have passed on to our students in the intervening years.

I have found these particular quotations especially helpful in trying to talk about what a poem is. Although intended for poetry as poetry, perhaps they can help us also understand how poetry can be prayer—especially how we might pray St. Francis' poem, "The Canticle of the Creatures."

> A good poem is the shortest distance between you and the subject.

I like this quote from Mark Van Doren, for people often think of a poem as a florid, over-written piece of writing that uses many words to say something that is actually quite simple. They base this misconception on many pseudo-poems, which are usually inferior imitations of earlier poems, whose language appears stilted, artificial, and dated, written by would-be poets who see poetry as decorative language.

The true poet writes in the language of the time and employs an economy of words—only those words needed to incarnate the poet's thought or experience. Even Walt Whitman, who runs on and on in cataloguing his experiences, is being selective as he heaps line upon line to create an effect of rich and abundant life.

The same economy must be true of prayer. Jesus tells us not to multiply words. "When you are praying, do not heap up empty phrases as the Gentiles do; for they think that they will be heard because of their many words. Do not be like them.... Pray then in this way" (Mt 6:7–9). And he then gives us the Our Father.

Like a good poem and its subject, a prayer is the shortest distance between the pray-er and God. Poetry teaches us how to revere words and make them matter, whether our words are brief like those of the Our Father or the poems of Emily Dickinson, or longer like those of the poems of Walt Whitman or some of the psalms. Making our words the shortest distance between God and what we want or need to say, keeps prayer honest and helps us to find our own voice, instead of padding our prayers with formulas that don't really express what we're feeling.

> We make out of the quarrel with others rhetoric, but
> of the quarrel with ourselves, poetry.

Poetry comes from that deep center where we are in conflict with ourselves, the place of contradictions, of opposing forces vying for sovereignty. Prayer's origins are the same. One could read St. Francis' "The Canticle of the Creatures" as a prayer-poem in which St. Francis sings of his reconciliation with all the opposites within him, embracing them in the end as complementary brothers and sisters of his soul, brothers and sisters *in* his soul.

Just as there is no art without conflict, without conflict prayer is sentimental. Conflict is of the essence of life. Prayer expresses the fullness of life. If there is no conflict, no tension in a prayer or in a poem, it somehow doesn't ring true.

The conflict need not be obvious; in fact, often the less obvious the conflict, the better. For example, on the surface, St. Francis' Canticle seems all light and joy and praise; and so it is—at first glance. Beneath that outer sheen is the inner work that went on in order for St. Francis to embrace all inner and outer creation as his brothers and sisters, and with them to praise God.

Like the authentic poem, authentic prayer is honest. It expresses the heart's doubts and fears, even about God. "Dear God, do you care?" for example, or "God, have you abandoned me?" True prayer is made of authentic not borrowed words, so that the formal prayers one chooses ring true to the pray-er's experience and illuminate her or his human stance before God. Thus, like a true poem, true prayer is both personally authentic and continuous with tradition—the prayers and formulations that have preceded it—that have risen from the deep conflicts of the human heart, prayers like those of Job, for example, or of Jesus on the cross crying out, "My God, my God, why have you forsaken me?" (Mt 27:46).

> Take a commonplace, clean and polish it, light it so that it produces the same effect of youth and freshness and spontaneity as it did originally, and you have done a poet's job.

6

Francis, illuminated by Jesus crucified,
is called to "rebuild my house."

Poets help us to see anew or for the first time something we took for granted or never noticed. As Wallace Stevens says, "A poet looks at the world as a man looks at a woman." *That* carefully, with *that* passion. The adjectives St. Francis uses for the different cosmic elements in "The Canticle of the Creatures" are evidence of this "new seeing." Sister Water, for example, is "chaste," a word we normally use for a person; and the stars are "precious," like gems. These adjectives derive not only from the way Francis sees, but from his depths where he has dreamed of the cosmic elements and given them values that reveal what they signify in his soul. St. Francis' words express the passion with which he sees. He is passionately in love with God and God's creation.

As Brother Thomas of Celano, his first biographer, says:

> St. Francis praised the Artist in every one of his works; whatever he found in things made, he referred to their Maker. He rejoiced in all the works of the Lord's hands, and with joyful vision saw into the reason and cause that gave them life. In beautiful things he came to know Beauty itself. To him all things were good. They cried out to him, "He who made us is infinitely good." By tracing his footprints in things, Francis followed

the Beloved wherever he led. He made, from created things, a ladder to his throne. [1]

Our prayer, like St. Francis' Canticle, needs to be something more than a cerebral, detached mouthing of words. It must come from the heart, from our passionate struggles, love, and desire for communion with God through all that God has made. Prayer, especially the prayer of contemplation, enables us to see anew.

> Poetry is the opening and closing of a door, leaving those who look through to guess what is seen during a moment.

There's something ineffable about real poetry *and* real prayer. Sandburg's metaphor of the opening and closing door echoes St. Paul's words, "What no eye has seen, nor ear heard, nor the human heart conceived, what God has prepared for those who love him—these things God has revealed to us through the Spirit" (1 Cor 2:9). Poetry is about words and how they can be doors into the unseen and unheard. It is about metaphorical language that opens briefly those worlds the heart longs for in prayer— the world of the Spirit; the world within the world we see with our physical eyes; the world as it is grasped by the imagination, which both creates and reveals realities the rational mind cannot define or reveal.

For the sake of a single poem, you must see many cities, many people and things, you must understand animals, must feel how birds fly, and know the gesture which small flowers make when they open in the morning.

St. Francis could only have written "The Canticle of the Creatures" at the end of his life. It is a poem that crystallizes a lifetime of reconciliation and integration, and is best described in these words of the great modern poet, Rainer Maria Rilke. Rilke also describes that mysterious process so central to art and to prayer, which St. Francis experienced in composing the "The Canticle of the Creatures":

> And it is not yet enough to have memories. You must be able to forget them when they are many, and you must have the immense patience to wait until they return. For the memories themselves are not important. Only when they have changed into our very blood, into glance and gesture, and are nameless, no longer to be distinguished from ourselves—only then can it happen that in some very rare hour the first word of a poem arises in their midst and goes forth from them.[2]

CHAPTER 2

The Life of St. Francis

St. Francis was so empty of nervous haste and fear and aggression that the birds would light on him.

—*Coleman Barks, English translator of Rumi*

Youth and Knighthood

Enter now the world of St. Francis, a medieval world of non-unified city-states warring among themselves for the surrounding lands. Francis was born in 1182 in the Umbrian town of Assisi, a walled city ruled at the time of his birth by the Holy Roman Emperor. His father Pietro Bernardone was a cloth merchant. His mother, Lady Pica, is said to have been a French woman whom Pietro probably met on one of his many buying trips in France. When the future saint was born, his father was away in France. Lady Pica had the boy baptized John, but when Pietro returned, he changed his name to Francesco, a nickname meaning, "the Frenchman." From the beginning, a tension surrounded this child who was twice named, symbolic of the struggle between father and mother for the child's soul—ultimately, a struggle between the father's world of commerce and greed and the mother's piety.

As the son of a wealthy man, Francis spent his youth in luxury, squandering money on clothes and parties. His generosity, combined with a quick wit and good humor, earned him the affection of his peers, who dubbed him "the king of revels." Francis loved to sing and dance, but his consuming ambition was to become a knight like his heroes, the legendary knight-errants of the court of King Arthur and the paladins of Charlemagne. His imagination was fired by the tales of these knights and their ladies, tales full of romance and chivalry which he heard sung by troubadours and their interpreters, the "jongleurs," who wandered the pilgrim routes visiting the cities.

Francis' dream of knighthood finally came true at the age of twenty when he rode off to fight in a war between Assisi and the neighboring city of Perugia. But his dreams were soon shattered when Assisi's forces were routed at the town of Ponte San Giovanni and Francis was taken prisoner. Instead of returning a victorious knight, he spent the following year in a Perugian prison. As time slowly passed, Francis covered his growing depression with attempted good humor; like the chivalrous knight of courage and courtesy, he tried to cheer his fellow prisoners even as his own health began to decline.

After a long year of complicated negotiations, Pietro was able to ransom his son. Francis returned to Assisi a broken man. He spent the next year, 1204, ill and in bed or hobbling about the rooms of his home. Medieval sources do not describe his illness as physical or psychological or both. We do know that in this time of forced interiority, Francis consoled himself with memories of his childhood when he was enchanted with all of nature, with feasting, extravagant clothes, and dancing through the streets by night.

With the coming of spring and the return of his strength, Francis ventured outside to walk in the fields of Assisi. He was shocked when even nature could not cheer him. So once again he opted for knighthood and battle— this time to escape his inner darkness. Perhaps a quest would again fire his mind and heart! With some fellow "knights," he set out for Apulia, south of Rome, to join the Papal forces under the command of the Norman captain, Gautier de Brienne. Again, Francis' plans were thwarted. He had ridden only as far Spoleto, a day's journey from Assisi, when he had the first of a series of dreams that would forever change his life.

While the bivouacked knights from Assisi slept, Francis dreamed of a large castle with a room whose walls were covered with shields. In his dream a voice proclaimed that the shields belonged to Francis and his "followers." The young dreamer took this as a prophecy that his goal of knightly glory was about to be fulfilled. But just as he was about to embrace knighthood as his life's work, he heard another voice:

"Francis, is it better to serve the Lord or the servant?"

"Why the Lord, of course."

"Then why are you trying to turn your Lord into a servant?"

Francis, realizing then that God was speaking to him, asked, "Lord, what do you want me to do?"

"Return to Assisi. There it shall be revealed to you what you are to do, and you will come to understand the meaning of this vision."

So in obedience to this voice, which Francis trusted was God's, he turned around and headed back to Assisi. Nothing could have been more humiliating for him than to return alone, a solitary knight who had apparently shrunk from the fight. But in the face of shame, Francis clung to God's word. He rode into Assisi not knowing what he was to do or say. This was to become a mark of his life: choosing to believe his voices and visions in the face of the greatest humiliations, and this incident was the first about-face Francis made in obedience to his voices and dreams.

Francis' Mission

The whole year after returning from Spoleto, Francis prayed, waiting for God's will to be revealed to him as his dream promised. He often spent time in a cave on Mount Subasio, the mountain that towers over Assisi, struggling with his demons. Thomas of Celano wrote of Francis' sojourns in the cave:

> He had a friend whom he loved more than the others. They were the same age and because of the intimacy of their mutual love, the man of God summoned the courage to share his secrets with him. He often took him to remote places where they could talk and told him that he had found a great and valuable treasure. This filled his friend with joy; and he was so excited about what he had heard, that he was glad to go with him whenever he was asked.
>
> They often went to a cave near the city where they talked about the treasure. The man of God, already holy because of his holy intention, would enter the cave while his friend waited outside. There, in-

*24-year old Francis publicly declares his loyalty to follow
the Lord, thus renouncing his family inheritance*

spired by a new and extraordinary spirit, he would pray to his *Father in secret*.... He prayed with all his heart that the eternal and true God would guide his way and *teach him to do his will*. His soul endured great suffering, and he couldn't rest until he accomplished what he had conceived in his heart. He was severely disturbed by relentless contrary thoughts. He burned inwardly with a divine fire and was unable to conceal outwardly the flame of his enkindled soul.

He repented for having sinned so grievously and for offending *the eyes of majesty*. And though he no longer found delight in past and present transgressions, he wasn't sure he could refrain from future ones. Therefore, when he came back out to his friend, he was so exhausted from his struggle that one person seemed to have entered, and another to have come out.[1]

In a brilliant analysis of this passage, the Franciscan, Eloi Leclerc, makes the following significant observations:

For St. Francis, as for the epic hero, in the depths of the cave there is always a precious treasure lying in wait for the one courageous and wise enough to seek it. Guarding the treasure, there is also a monster of some kind with whom the hero must battle. To bury oneself in the cave is, therefore, to accept struggle, fear, and death.

The dark depths are those of the soul; the cavern is the archetypal image relating the soul to its own archeology and that of humankind, past and present. Thus, a new wholeness, a further integration, is achieved each time one enters the cavern of the soul to do battle with whatever monsters are preventing one from attaining the treasure.[2]

A natural gift for music and the capacity for vision Francis already had, but the making of the poet and the saint began in earnest with the archetypal gesture of entering the cave and emerging again. When Francis entered the cave, he also entered into his soul, the inexhaustible source of the transformed images that he would take with him the rest of his life. In his soul he heard the Gospel, he meditated on the images that rose from the Gospel stories, and he wondered how and when he would begin to live the Gospel that had become the poetic landscape of his meditative soul.

The answer came one day while Francis was riding his horse on a road below Assisi. Suddenly, a leper stood there before him on the road. Instinctively, Francis reined in his horse and attempted to turn and ride in the opposite direction in fear and disgust at the sight of the disfigured person. But something in his Gospel-touched inner landscape stopped his retreat. He dismounted his horse, walked up to the leper, and placed coins in his hands. Then, in a gesture he did not fully understand, Francis embraced the leper.

This incident was so important in Francis' life that he placed it at the very beginning of his Last Testament, which he composed for his brothers many years later, when his health began to fail: "For, I, being in sins, thought it bitter to look at lepers, and the Lord himself led me among them, and I worked mercy with them. And when I left their company, I realized that what had seemed bitter to me, had been turned into sweetness of soul and body."[3]

When Francis mounted his horse, he turned to wave to the leper, but saw no one on the road. He knew then that he had seen and embraced the Savior himself, and he realized that if he would know Jesus Christ, he would have to seek out the lepers who lived in the swamp-like conditions of the plain below the city. He also knew that clarity regarding his mission would come only after intense daily prayer to further discern the will of God. And so Francis began to pray in the poor, neglected churches outside the city walls, hoping to find there the poor, neglected Savior of the Gospel.

One day, Francis was praying before the crucifix in the dilapidated chapel of San Damiano. He was looking intently at the crucifix when he heard the Voice he had heard once before in his dream: "Francis, go and repair my house which, as you see, is falling into ruins."

Francis' response was immediate and literal. He rushed home, took a bolt of cloth from his father's shop, and rode off to the neighboring town of Foligno, where he sold the cloth and his father's horse. He returned to San Damiano and offered the money to the priest and told him it was for the repair of the church. The priest, however, was suspicious. Here was the son of the richest man in Assisi. Did his father know what Francis was doing? Did he approve? He feared Pietro's wrath if this was yet another of his son's rash acts. He refused the money. Disappointed, Francis flung the money on the windowsill of the chapel and climbed the hill toward Assisi to gather stones to repair the church himself.

Poetry is revealed both in the act of embracing the leper and in rebuilding San Damiano. Francis' gestures become symbols of a deeper reality, much as a verbal metaphor holds more meaning than it first appears. When Francis embraced the leper, he simultaneously embraced Christ, and in embracing Christ, he embraced the entire

Mystical Body of Christ. For, as St. Paul wrote so beautifully, "If one member suffers, all suffer together with it; if one member is honored, all rejoice together with it. Now you are the body of Christ and individually members of it" (1 Cor 12:26–27).

When Francis began to rebuild the chapel of San Damiano by laying one stone on another, this became a symbol of that other rebuilding, which would restore the Church itself. The real stones that Francis began with would, in time, become the living stones of Francis' followers: "Come to him, a living stone, though rejected by mortals yet chosen and precious in God's sight, and like living stones, let yourselves be built into a spiritual house, to be a holy priesthood, to offer spiritual sacrifices acceptable to God through Jesus Christ" (1 Pt 2:4–5). Like a true poet, Francis always began with concrete things such as stones, and his work with them made of them symbols of an inner reality that was not immediately evident, a sacramental gesture that characterized his entire life.

Francis and His Father

Now, while Francis set about repairing the chapel of San Damiano and begging for food through the streets of Assisi, his father Pietro was away. When he returned, Pietro was confronted with rumors that his son had gone

Francis and his fledgling community receive ecclesiastical approval by Pope Innocent III

mad, was playing the fool, and was living at San Damiano. Enraged and grieved by this dishonor to the family name, Pietro went in search of his son. He dragged Francis back to the family home and chained him in a small cell until he should come to his senses. But when business matters called Pietro away, Francis' mother broke his chains and released the young man, who immediately returned to San Damiano.

This conflict between Pietro and Lady Pica over Francis had an unconscious effect on Francis himself. Lady Pica's maternal instinct freed Francis from Pietro's chains, but she also began to break the chains of Francis' desire for knighthood and the violence of war that had held him prisoner. With each successive break the poet and saint began to emerge.

The scene precipitated by Pietro's return to Assisi is one of the most famous in the Franciscan story. The father, enraged by his wife's betrayal and his son's intransigence, reviled Lady Pica and set off to bring his son home. However, by this time Francis was steeled by prayer. When Pietro arrived at San Damiano, Francis told his father he was no longer afraid of chains or imprisonment or beating; he was ready to endure anything for the love of Christ.

Frustrated, Pietro returned home determined to at least force some compensation from his son for the stolen cloth and horse. He went to the town officials, who sent a town crier to summon Francis. But Francis refused the summons, declaring that as God's servant he was no longer under civil jurisdiction. The bishop of Assisi intervened and summoned Francis to appear before him. Francis consented, saying, "I will appear before the bishop for he is the father and master of souls."

The scene was set. Francis re-entered the walled city of Assisi and appeared before his father, the bishop, and the assembled citizens. Not only did he return his father's money, but, stripping himself before everyone, he laid his clothes at his father's feet. As Bishop Guido covered Francis' nakedness with his own cloak, the young man turned to his father and the crowd and said, "Up to now I have called Pietro Bernardone my father! But now that I am determined to serve God, I give him back not only this money that he wants so much, but all the clothes I have from him! From now on, I can advance naked before the Lord, saying in truth no longer: my father, Pietro Bernardone, but our Father who art in Heaven!" It was 1206, and Francis was twenty-four years old.

In this public renunciation of his father, Francis became the prophet and troubadour of a world other than the one he had known in his family. He was very much aware that his actions would cause others to scrutinize him for sincerity or madness. He would be held accountable for his words. He had proclaimed God alone as his Father and he was henceforth forced to face the implications of living out such a dramatic utterance. Francis the poet once again enacted a metaphor; the son of a cloth merchant used his unclothing as a symbol of renouncing his father's values.

And so Francis walked out of the town of Assisi and began his life as a poor, itinerant man, like his Savior. He felt a freedom and joy of heart reminiscent of his youth, before war and imprisonment in Perugia, before his illness. He set out immediately to visit a friend in the town of Gubbio, perhaps the same friend who had accompanied him to the cave on Mount Subasio.

The pattern and rhythm of what can be called his first missionary journey became another model for Francis' life. Because he was sent by voices and visions that had inspired his decision to embrace God as his all, his gestures seemed foolishness to those who failed to understand how fully he embraced the wisdom of the cross.

This seeming folly was tested almost as soon as his journey began.

As he walked along toward Gubbio, he was intercepted by robbers who were after the money he no longer had. Disappointed and angered, they threw him into a ditch. Francis rose singing that he had nothing anyone could take from him, that he was considered worthless, that he had no goods to defend. At that moment, he became the Gospel person fallen among thieves; in the future he would reach down into the ditches along the roads he traveled, pull out those fallen or cast away, and minister to their wounds. Francis eventually called himself a brother of penance. He embraced all of creation as his brother and sister, and that embrace was penitential because it included all of creation, even the repulsive.

His own daily experiences became Gospel metaphors for Francis, because he saw the actions of Christ's life everywhere. He walked into water, and it was holy because Christ said that he is living water and because Christ was baptized by John in the Jordan River. The earth Francis walked on was holy because Christ walked upon the earth. Air was holy because Christ breathed it; fire was holy because Christ said he was a living flame who came to cast fire upon the earth.

The Franciscan Mission Grows

When Francis returned from Gubbio, he went to San Damiano to continue rebuilding the church. Others joined Francis; the first were Bernard of Quintavalle, a leading citizen of Assisi, and Peter Catani, a lawyer. They gave away all their possessions to join Francis in following the footsteps of the poor Christ. When the poor brothers were twelve in number, they walked to Rome where Pope Innocent III approved their "way of life," which at that time consisted mainly of Gospel injunctions meant to guide the life of the brothers. From there, they went forth to the world to witness to the Gospel by living in poverty, chastity, and obedience as itinerant preachers of penance.

From those humble beginnings the followers of Francis grew to over 5,000 during his lifetime. Women, too, embraced this way of radical poverty. The first was Clare, a noble woman of Assisi, who was received by Francis and the brothers and to whom Bishop Guido entrusted San Damiano, the church Francis restored with his own hands. There, Clare and her followers established an Order of Poor Ladies; like the brothers, they lived their lives in imitation of the poor Christ and his mother Mary. The Poor Ladies devoted themselves to prayer and contemplation, and the brothers went through the world preach-

One of Francis' most famous mystical experiences—
a vision of ascending to heaven in a flaming chariot

ing, singing devotional songs and teaching them to the people, and modeling their lives after Christ.

Gradually, Francis himself became more and more a contemporary icon of the poor Jesus. He centered his life and his preaching on the crib, the cross, and the Eucharist, dramatizing in his own life each of these mysteries of the Incarnation. In 1223, for example, three years before he died, Francis told his brothers that he wanted to celebrate the feast of Christmas in a new way. He and a few of the brothers went to the town of Greccio above the Rieti valley, halfway between Rome and Assisi. There, high on a hillside, where today a Franciscan hermitage perches precariously, Francis sent word to the people of the village of Greccio. Carrying torches, they came at midnight to a little cave on a hillside opposite the village. They celebrated Christmas mass around a small stone altar where an ox and ass stood watch as had once happened at the birth of the baby Jesus. As Francis proclaimed the Gospel and preached, a man named John of Vellita saw the infant Jesus appear as if in the manger of Bethlehem. Francis' metaphorical re-enactment of the meaning of a Gospel event began the tradition of the live Christmas crèche and the popularization of the Christmas crib.

That God was revealed in human flesh was to Francis a constant source of awe: God a baby, a carpenter, an accused criminal hanging on the cross, the risen God-Man in the Eucharist. So dear was the Incarnation to Francis that—almost unbelievably for the man of penance—he told his brothers that if the feast of Christmas fell on a Friday, a day of abstaining from meat, not only were they to eat meat, but they were to rub meat on the walls in honor of the Incarnation, the enfleshment of God among us!

The story of the crucified Christ in Francis' life and preaching was nowhere more dramatically rendered than in the sacred stigmata, which Francis received the year after the Christmas celebration at Greccio. Francis, malnourished and seriously ill with tuberculosis, and suffering from a disease that caused hemorrhaging of his eyes, made the long journey by foot to Mount La Verna, far to the north of Assisi. He went on pilgrimage to prepare for the Feast of the Exaltation of the Holy Cross and the Feast of St. Michael the Archangel, to whom Francis had a deep devotion.

There on the heights of La Verna, Francis was sealed body and soul with the wounds of Christ in an ecstatic vision, becoming an image of the crucified Savior. During the remaining two years of his life he endeavored to modestly conceal the wounds, because they were such a public sign of something intimately private: his union with Christ.

For Francis, the Eucharist was the incarnation of the risen Christ. Nowhere did he see his resurrected Lord more unequivocally than in the Holy Eucharist. One chapter of his final Rule, approved by Pope Honorius III in 1223, was devoted to the Eucharistic Lord, as was his entire First Admonition to his brothers.

In medieval times a religious "admonition" consisted of a Biblical passage that was given a practical application. Francis adhered to this tradition, opening the First Admonition with three Scripture quotations and then a commentary on the Holy Eucharist.

The father "dwells in unapproachable light" (1 Tm 6:16), and "No one has ever seen God" (Jn 1:18). Because God is Spirit, he can be seen only in the Spirit; for "it is the spirit that gives life, the flesh is useless" (Jn 6:63). Likewise, neither is the Son, in that he is equal to the Father, seen by anyone but the Father and the Holy Spirit. Therefore, all who saw the Lord Jesus Christ and did not believe, in the Spirit, that he was divine, the true Son of God, were condemned.

And so, too, now, all who see the sacrament of the Body of Christ, which is consecrated by the words of the Lord upon the altar in the hands of the priest in the form of bread and wine, and do not see and do not believe in the Spirit, that it is divine, indeed, the Most Holy Body and Blood of our Lord Jesus Christ, are condemned, because the Most High himself gives witness and says, "This is my body, and the blood of the covenant" (cf. Mk 14:22, 24).[4]

When Francis returned to Assisi from La Verna, he continued for two more years to witness to Christ among the lepers, the poor, and all who would listen to his words. Francis died on October 3, 1226, singing the final stanza of the Canticle in which he welcomed Sister Death.

The whole trajectory of Francis' life is that of one who was wholly in love with Jesus Christ. The way he responded to God's love for him was unique, as he indicated in his final gesture and words to his brothers. Covering the wound in his side, he said, "I have done what was mine to do; may the Lord show you what is yours to do".[5]

CHAPTER 3

Francis the Poet

His Poetry and Ideals

Francis of Assisi—lover of nature, the little poor man who spoke to the birds, who tamed the wolf of Gubbio, who called all creatures his brothers and sisters, the saint, mystic, and poet—began his journey longing to become a knight and ending up a troubadour of God. In the tradition of the troubadours of Languedoc, he sang a "swan song" at the end of his life, his great poem, "The Canticle of the Creatures."

Because he was a poet, Francis *sang* the praises of God; and when he was particularly moved, his fondness for the French language won out. Thomas of Celano writes:

> When the sweetest melody of spirit would bubble up in him, he would give exterior expression to it in French, and the breath of the divine whisper which his ear perceived in secret would burst forth in French in a song of joy. At times...he would pick up a stick from the ground and putting it over his left arm, would

draw across it, as across a violin, a little bow bent by means of a string; and going through the motions of playing, he would sing in French about his Lord. The whole ecstasy of joy would often end in tears and his song of gladness would be dissolved in compassion for the passion of Christ.[1]

Francis was so imbued with the songs of the troubadours and the language of Sacred Scripture, which he said he knew by heart, that when he spoke, the words that filled his mind and imagination poured out in poetic, ecstatic utterance. Read, for example, his "Praises of God," written after receiving the sacred stigmata for his beloved Brother Leo, his confessor, scribe, and constant companion during Francis' last years. (On the poem's parchment, Brother Leo marked in red ink that Blessed Francis wrote these praises in his own hand.)

You are holy, Lord,
God alone,
who work marvels.
You are strong.
You are grand.
You are Most High.
You are the All-Powerful King,

You, Holy Father,
King of heaven and earth.
You are three and one,
Lord God of gods.
You are the Good,
every good,
the highest good,
the Lord God, living and true.
You are love, charity.
You are wisdom.
You are humility.
You are patience.
You are beauty.
You are safety.
You are rest.
You are joy and gladness.
You are our hope.
You are our justice.
You are temperance.
You are all our treasure overflowing.
You are beauty.
You are meekness.
You are our protector.

You are our guardian and defender.
You are strength.
You are refreshment.
You are our hope.
You are our faith.
You are our charity.
You are all our sweetness.
You are our eternal life,
great and wondrous Lord,
God All-Powerful,
merciful Savior.[2]

The language is simple and direct, and the rhythm and technique are those of the psalms in the repetition, litany-like reinforcement, and cataloguing of God's attributes. One can imagine St. Francis singing these words and accompanying himself with an imaginary violin.

Francis' "Perfect Joy"

St. Francis was not just a singer of poetry, however. There is also poetry in the way he lived and preached, inspired as he was by the chivalric ideals of his time. A good example is his parable of perfect joy, found in *The Little Flowers of St. Francis*, a collection of stories and legends surrounding the life of Francis and his followers.

Francis and Brother Leo were on the road from Perugia to St. Mary of the Angels, their poor dwelling on the plain below Assisi. Francis took the opportunity to instruct Brother Leo with the parable of "perfect joy."

After describing what perfect joy is not, Francis imagined "perfect joy": the rejection and beating they would receive from the brother porter of St. Mary of the Angels, who, not recognizing Francis and Leo when they arrive, would send them away. In Francis' vision, they repeatedly return and knock and are sent away, until finally "the brother storms out with a knotty club, and grabbing us by the cowl, hurls us onto the ground, rolling us in the mud and snow, beating us so savagely that our bodies are covered with wounds. If we endure that evil and the insults and blows with joy reflecting that we must accept and bear the sufferings of the Blessed Christ patiently for love of him, O Brother Leo, write: this is Perfect Joy!"[3]

Here, St. Francis recalled the true knight, tested by the rejection of his beloved, yet so rooted in what the troubadours called *fin'amor* (purified love) that he retains his composure and love. Likewise, the true friar, though rejected and beaten by his brother, retains his fraternal composure and love because of his love for the Beloved. And *that* is perfect joy.

Francis' "little brothers" were often witnesses
to his ecstasy during prayer

How can we understand this "perfect joy," which sounds so much like "perfect humiliation"? One way to understand "perfect joy" is through the Gospel paradoxes of losing life in order to find it, of dying in order to live. Yet, in order to get the full flavor of Francis' story, it is helpful to know something of the tradition of courtly love, which began at the Court of Poitier in eleventh-century France.

Simply put, courtly love is a kind of secular religion meant to humanize and regulate a man's devotion to a beautiful and virtuous lady, whose reciprocal love ennobles the man who woos her. The "demands" of this religion require that the lover sing of a lady to whom he is forever dedicated; the lady's requital must be earned by sustained service; and finally, the lady must be unattainable because of her noble birth, her accomplishments and virtues…and sometimes, because she is already married. In service of his lady, the knight strives to be evermore skillful at arms while remaining humble and noble in his bearing.

One of the last European troubadours, Jaufre Rudel, introduced *amor de lonh*, love from afar, which was more perfect than requited love. In the Italy of Francis' time *amor de lonh* was transformed into spiritual songs about a lady who seemed angelic and who would lead the "lover" to salvation. In the songs of the Church, this lady-figure became the Virgin Mary, the quintessentially unattainable woman. For Dante, she was Beatrice, a woman who died before he could declare his own undying love, but who continued to be his transforming muse. And for St. Francis she was Lady Poverty, the Gospel virtue of holy poverty enfleshed in a fictional woman, the symbolic Bride of Christ, whom St. Francis and the brothers took as their transforming lover.

Franciscan Allegory: Francis and Lady Poverty

To understand anyone, it is important to understand the milieu in which they lived: the songs they sang, the clothes they wore, the stories they heard, the way the sun rose and set over the place where they were born and the place where they died. Allegory may seem awkward to us, but it was the literary convention of lords and ladies of the twelfth and thirteenth centuries, and tales of knighthood, chivalry and courtly love were their "romance novels." Allegory conveys truth through symbolic, fictionalized characters, offering an incarnational way of looking at reality. Like sacrament, allegory is holistic; it does not separate the spiritual and material, but fuses them together.

Francis, like the young men of every age, internalized the values of his age. He was a medieval merchant's son, a poet formed by the poems he heard. For Francis, allegory was a natural way of looking at the world, a "tangible" way of contemplation. Francis spoke of the Gospel ideal of poverty as "Lady Poverty"; he called St. Clare and her Sisters at San Damiano the "Poor Ladies," as was fitting for those who were brides of the Lord "of the castle of San Damiano," Jesus Christ. In this way, Francis created an allegory in which he and his brothers were knights-errant traveling the roads of the world, doing heroic deeds under the banner of the Poor Ladies of "the castle of San Damiano," women who were perfect personifications of Lady Poverty.

Somewhere between 1237 and 1239, an anonymous allegorical tale appeared entitled "The Sacred Exchange between St. Francis and Lady Poverty," which expressed St. Francis' dedication to the Gospel paradox of poverty and joy. This allegory took abstract, spiritual ideas such as *poverty and avarice*, and incarnated them in flesh-and-blood human characters. Its main protagonist is Lady Poverty, for whom Francis is pining like a love-stuck troubadour. In the story, Francis meets two elderly men and begs them, "Tell me, where does Lady Poverty live, where does she eat, where does she lie at midday, for I am faint with love for her?" The men reply that she has gone up "into the mountain where God has led her." Furthermore, the way to find her is to "remove the garments of your rejoicing and take with you a few faithful companions that you may listen to their help and be strengthened by their advice."

Francis and his brothers ascend the mountain in search of Lady Poverty and eventually bring her down to their dwelling on the plain. They offer her a "banquet" of a few bread crusts and a vessel of cold water; afterward, Lady Poverty lies down upon the bare ground with a stone for a pillow. When she awakens, she asks the brothers to show her their cloister. They bring her to a hill and show her the whole world, proclaiming, "This, Lady, is our cloister!" She blesses them and declares, "Today I was with you in the Paradise of God."

The allegory's "descent in order to ascend," along with the hints of "stripping in order to clothe" and "renouncing in order to possess," demonstrate the essential paradox of "perfect joy" in the Franciscan tradition. Lady Poverty ends the *Sacred Exchange* by describing the virtues of those who have found "perfect joy," and declares, "My soul is joined fast with theirs, and there is one spirit and one faith in us."

Dante spelled out the allegory of Francis and Lady Poverty in his own exquisite poetry of the "Paradiso," the final book of *The Divine Comedy*.

> While still a youth he braved his father's wrath,
> because he loved a lady to whom all
> would bar the door as if to death itself.
>
> Before the bishop's court *et coram patre*
> he took this lady as his lawful wife;
> from day to day he loved her more.
>
> Bereft of her first spouse, despised, ignored
> she waited eleven hundred years and more,
> living without a lover till he came,…
>
> In plain words
> take Francis, now, and Poverty to be
> the lovers in the story I have told.[4]

St. Francis himself wrote lovingly of Lady Poverty in some of his early songs. Though none of these survive, an expression of his devotion may be found in the songs of the troubadour poets, such as this one by Bernart de Ventadour:

> I may go about without clothes,
> naked in my shirt—

"I want to see with my own eyes the poverty in which
Christ our King was born." (Francis of Assisi)

perfect love protects me from the chill wind.
The more fool is he who does things out of
    measure
and doesn't hold himself with courtesy;
But I have taken thought with myself,
from the time when I begged
the most beautiful for her love,
from which I expect so much good
that in exchange for these riches
I would not take all of Pisa.[5]

These words could easily have been sung by Francis of Assisi. They reveal the root of the perfect joy created in his life by his marriage with the Spouse of Christ, Lady Poverty. As St. Francis said early in his conversion, "I am going to espouse a more noble and beautiful lady than you have ever seen; she will surpass all others in beauty and wisdom".[6]

The embrace of Lady Poverty defined the brothers and sealed, as a marriage vow, their lifelong commitment to Gospel poverty, desired by Jesus in three passages of Holy Scripture that the brothers received from the priest of the Church of St. Nicholas in Assisi. St. Francis and his first companions, Bernard of Quintavalle and Peter Catani, had asked the priest to open the Gospels for them three times and read aloud the passages God would give them as their way of life. And this is what was read:

> "If you wish to be perfect, go, sell your possessions, and give the money to the poor" (Mt 19:21).

> "Take nothing for your journey" (Lk 9:3).

> "If any want to become my followers, let them deny themselves and take up their cross and follow me" (Mt 16:24).

Upon hearing this Word from God, Francis declared, "This is our life and our rule." How severe this radical poverty, this cross sounds to us! But in the context of medieval knighthood and courtly love, there is romance underneath it all…and "perfect joy" besides!

St. Francis' Philosophy and Theology

In keeping with the sciences of his day, St. Francis sang of earth, water, air, and fire as the cosmic and psychological elements of which all things were made. For medieval people, "creation" was a universe with the earth at its center. Some believed that hell was at the center of the earth and that it was reached by a tunnel, beside which rose the mountain of Purgatory.

In the air that surrounded the earth dwelled spirits, both evil and good. Beyond this air was the ether, the home of the Angels, and where the moon and six other planets circled the earth: Mercury, Venus, the Sun, Mars, Jupiter, and Saturn. Beyond the ether was the realm of the stars and the galaxies which, unlike the planets, were fixed. The last dimension of time and space was a rotating void. Beyond time and space was the *empyrean*, the infinite and eternal realm of God which surrounded the whole system of the created universe. Here God dwelled, Father, Son, and Holy Spirit, together with Mary, Queen of Heaven, and the hierarchy of Cherubim, Seraphim, Thrones, Virtues, Dominions, Powers, Principalities, Archangels, and Angels.[7]

Such a cosmology placed God high above the universe and lifted human eyes heavenward when praying or invoking the name of God. St. Francis prayed this way, too, but he also directed his eyes horizontally to all of the works of the Most High God on planet earth. Though St. Francis moved toward the Most High, he did so through the visible signs of God in creation. It is extraordinary that Francis prayed this way, because he lived at a time when the Albigensian heresy strongly influenced the way people saw the world. Albigensianism claims that there are two gods: a good god who creates the soul, and an evil god who creates the body and the material world. Therefore, all creation is divided between the good spiritual world and the evil material world. The Albigensians even rejected the sacraments as vehicles of grace because of their material elements—bread, wine, water, oil, consummated love.

Instead, Francis celebrated all of creation because of his belief in Jesus Christ. In Christ, God was made known, and in Christ all of creation was subsumed, for he was the firstborn of all creation, the fullness of everything God had made: the entire material universe spoke of Christ. This Christocentric concept was given a unique interpretation in the theology of the Franciscan, Blessed John Duns Scotus. For Scotus, the Incarnation of the Second Person of the Trinity does not depend upon the sin of Adam. Christ did not come among us as a man *because we had sinned*, rather, he chose to assume our human nature *even though* we had sinned.

Christ, according to Scotus, is the first intention in the mind of the Creator conceiving creation. Christ is willed in himself and not as someone to repair the damage done by sin.

Scripture expresses it thus:

> He is the image of the invisible God, the firstborn of all creation; for in him all things in heaven and on earth were created, things visible and invisible, whether thrones or dominions or rulers or powers—all things have been created through him and for him. He himself is before all things, and in him all things hold together. He is the head of the body, the church; he is the beginning, the firstborn from the dead, so that he might come to have first place in everything. For in him all the fullness of God was pleased to dwell, and through him God was pleased to reconcile to himself all things, whether on earth or in heaven, by making peace through the blood of his cross (Col 1:15–20).

Christ died and made peace through his death on the cross because human nature itself is tainted by sin and death. Yet, even if it were not, he still would have come to take possession of all creation. Christ shares in everything created, even death, though not in the sin that caused death.

For St. Francis, as for us, there was something freeing in the belief that the Incarnation was not dependent on the negative reality of sin, that Christ would have come even if Adam and Eve had not sinned, because for his sake all things in heaven and earth were created in love.

No wonder St. Francis delighted in all created things. In his *Life of St. Francis*, St. Bonaventure writes,

> He delighted in all the works of God's hands and from an earthly vision of joy his mind soared heavenward to the life-giving source and cause of it all. In every-thing beautiful, he saw the One who is beauty itself, and by his likeness imprinted on creation, he followed his Beloved everywhere. Of all creation he made a ladder by which he could ascend and embrace the One who is all-desirable.
>
> By the power of his extraordinary faith he tasted, as in so many rivulets, the Goodness which is the source of everything in each created thing. He seemed to perceive a divine harmony in the interplay of pow-ers and faculties given by God to his creatures and like the prophet David he exhorted them all to praise God.[8]

For St. Francis, to sing of creation was to sing of Christ. Though never mentioned by name, Christ is found throughout the Canticle because he is in all creation: Christ is in fact the fullness of creation.

St. Francis and his Brothers embraced the sufferings of Christ with joy, through the transformational embrace of Lady Poverty. For those who will take up his cross and follow him, the resurrected Christ's sufferings are turned into eternal joy and his passage into creation restores all of creation to its Eden-like character. It is this restored creation that St. Francis celebrates in his "Canticle of the Creatures."

St. Francis' whole life was a metaphor of the poor, crucified Christ. His contemporaries called him the mirror of Christ, so closely did the gestures of his own life conform to the public life of Jesus, even as he followed Christ as a man of his own times, using the imagery and language of the troubadours, the posture of the true knight. St. Francis was a medieval Christian whose living out of the Gospel became a poem that people could read. And they read there the Gospel of Jesus Christ come to life in their world.

CHAPTER 4

The Canticle of St. Francis

Poetry of Praise

Although St. Francis' whole being was that of a poet, he was not a poet in the modern sense of someone whose vocation or avocation is the writing of poetry. St. Francis' vocation was to follow in the footsteps of Jesus Christ by living in poverty, chastity, and obedience, but he walked and praised as a poet would as he followed Jesus, singing aloud his spontaneous songs of joy and sorrow. He stored up in his heart the images of earth, water, air, and fire that poured forth toward the end of his life in his "Canticle of the Creatures."

There are other writings of St. Francis that partake of the rhythm and imagery of poetry. He composed hymns to the virtues, the Blessed Virgin Mary, the Most High God; and he composed an Office of the Passion in which he chose lines from the psalms and combined them into new poems that imagine Christ as a hero. But of all his writings "The Canticle of the Creatures," sometimes called "The Canticle of Brother Sun," most clearly reveals and expresses Francis' poetic soul.

A Canticle is usually a religious song, which calls to mind those of Solomon, Zechariah, and Mary found in Scripture. It is a song of praise and joy like Psalm 148:

Praise the LORD!
Praise the LORD from the heavens;
praise him in the heights!
Praise him, all his angels;
praise him, all his host!

Praise him, sun and moon;
praise him, all you shining stars!…

Praise the LORD from the earth,
you sea monsters and all deeps,
fire and hail, snow and frost,
stormy wind fulfilling his command!

Mountains and all hills,
fruit trees and all cedars!
Wild animals and all cattle,
creeping things and flying birds!…

Praise the LORD!

In the Middle Ages, a Canticle was sometimes called a *Lauda,* a praise song, and was the vernacular equivalent or adaptation of a Latin hymn. There is evidence that St. Francis did in fact sing the Canticle, perhaps to an original melody or a troubadour melody or, as some believe, to the melody of the *Exultet* sequence of the Holy Saturday liturgy.

The oldest manuscript of the Canticle, dated 1279 and preserved in the Sacro Convento of the Basilica of St. Francis in Assisi, has spaces between the lines that are wide enough for musical notes to be included. If they were ever written down, they have yet to be found. We do know that St. Francis sang or recited his Canticle in the Umbrian dialect, thereby creating one of the first great Italian poems. Truly, it can only be fully appreciated in its original form, because the nuances, rhythms, and sounds of a great poem are the most exquisite articulation of its native language.

St. Francis' Canticle is written in rhythmical prose that uses assonance (the repetition of vowel sounds) instead of rhyme. These vowel sounds are particularly difficult to render in English. For example, the large, open vowels of the Italian words used for God in the first two stanzas, contrast with the small, constricted vowels used

Francis preaches to the birds—praising God the Creator for all his gifts of nature and grace

for creatures in the third stanza. However, even in English, we can still glimpse the images, the depths, and the rhythms of the original.

The movement of the Canticle is that of the quest. The object of this quest, its "Holy Grail," is the "Most High, all-powerful, good Lord." The poet's outward journey into all of creation is really a journey into the soul. Before considering the details, let us read the whole poem.

Altissimu, omnipotente, bonsignore,
tue sono le laude,
la gloria elhonore
et omne benedictione.

Most High, all-powerful, good Lord,
yours is the praise,
the glory and the honor
and every blessing.

Ad te solo, Altissimo, se Konfano
et nullu homo enne dignu
te mentovare.

They belong to you alone, Most High,
and no one is worthy
to speak your name.

Laudato sie, misignore, cum tucte le tue creature,
spetialmente messor lo frate sole,
loquale iorno et allumini noi par loi.

Praised be you, my Lord, with all your creatures,
especially Sir Brother Sun,
who makes the day and enlightens us through you.

Et ellu ebellu eradiante cum grande splendore:
de te, Altissimo, porta significatione.

And he is lovely, shining with great splendor
for he heralds you, Most High.

Laudato si', misignore, per sora luna ele stelle:
in celu lai formate clarite
et pretiose et belle.

Praised be you, my Lord,
    through Sister Moon and Stars.
You have formed them in heaven, lightsome
and precious and fair.

Laudato si', misignore, per frate vento,
et per aere et nubilo
et sereno et omne tempo
per loquale a le tue creature
dai sustentamento.

Praised be you, my Lord, through Brother Wind,
through air and cloud,
and calm and every weather
through which you sustain your creatures.

Laudato si', misignore, per sor aqua
laquale e multo utile et humile
et pretiosa et casta.

Praised be you, my Lord, through Sister Water,
so very useful and humble
and precious and chaste.

Laudato si', misignore, per frate focu,
per loquale ennalumini la nocte
edello ebello et jocundo
et robustoso et forte.

Praised be you, my Lord, through Brother Fire,
through whom you illumine our night.
And he is handsome and merry,
robust and strong.

Laudato si', misignore, per sora nostra matre terra,
laquale ne sustenta et governa
et produce diversi fructi
con coloriti flori et herba.

Praised be you, my Lord, through our Sister,
   Mother Earth.
In her sovereignty she nourishes us,
bringing forth all kinds of fruits
and colored flowers and herbs.

These first stanzas constitute the original, sustained song that rose from the depths of St. Francis' soul; he later added six more stanzas. At the time of their singing, he was prostrate with illness in a small hut next to the monastery of the Poor Ladies. He had descended from Mount LaVerna more than fifty days before, hemorrhaging from the wounds of the stigmata, almost blind, and weakened from malnutrition. In addition, he felt profoundly depressed by the direction the Order he founded was taking. He felt the brothers were betraying Lady Poverty by building houses and living more comfortably than a poor follower of Jesus Christ should.

St. Francis lay on the ground in the dark, unable to bear the light of the sun or a lamp without his eyes beginning to hemorrhage. Field mice ran over his emaciated body. Then, in the middle of this dark night of the soul and the senses, while he was praying in great agony, he heard a voice in spirit:

"Tell me, Brother, if, in compensation for your sufferings and tribulations you were given an immense and precious treasure: the whole mass of earth changed into pure gold, pebbles into precious stones, and the water of the rivers into perfume, would you not regard the pebbles and the waters as nothing compared to such a treasure? Would you not rejoice?"

Blessed Francis answered: "Lord, it would be a very great, very precious, an inestimable treasure beyond all else that one can love and desire!" "Well, Brother," the voice said, "be glad and joyful in the midst of your infirmities and tribulations: as of now, live in peace as if you were already sharing my kingdom."[1]

Francis realized that his sufferings had been so closely united to those of his Savior that now the earth, restored by the touch of his resurrected Lord, was his. As reflected in many medieval lives of the saints, Francis' journey is that of the redeemed Adam who, through penance and love of God and neighbor, attains a new, redeemed relationship to the created world. He could not hold back his joy. He broke into song—his "Canticle of the Creatures"—which became more than a poem about the resurrected earth. The external world became a map of Francis' own internal world.

Reconciliation in the Canticle

Some time after the singing of the original stanzas of the Canticle, there was a dispute between the mayor and the bishop of Assisi. St. Francis composed an additional two stanzas and asked one of the Brothers to sing them before the two men so that they would be reconciled. A reconciliation did occur, indicating that St. Francis knew the deeper significance and power of the poem beyond what its simple words may lead the reader to believe.

Laudato si', misignore, per quelli ke perdonano
per lo tuo amore
et sostengo infirmitate
et tribulatione.

Praised be you, my Lord,
for those who forgive
in your love
and who bear sickness
and trial.

Beati quelli kel sosterrano in pace,
ka da te, Altissimo,
sirano incoronati.

Blessed are those who endure in peace,
for by you, Most High,
they will be crowned.

Then, shortly before he died, St. Francis sang the final stanzas of the Canticle, in which he welcomed death as his sister.

Laudato si', misignore, per sora nostra
morte corporale,
da laquale nullo homo
vivente poskappare.

Praised be you, my Lord, through our Sister
Bodily Death
from whom no living being
can escape.

Guai aqueli ke morrano
ne le peccata mortali!

How dreadful for those who die
in mortal sin!

Beati quelli ke trovara ne
ne le sanctissime voluntati,
ka la morte secunda
nol farra male.

*As Francis prays, a miraculous spring appears,
providing water for a man dying of thirst*

How blessed are those who are found
in your most holy will,
for the second death
can do them no harm.

Laudate et benedicite, misignore,
et rengratiate et serviate li
cum grande humilitate.

Praise and bless my Lord,
thank him and serve him
humbly but grandly!

The whole Canticle, comprised of only fifteen stanzas, constitutes one of the greatest medieval poems and establishes St. Francis of Assisi as one of the premier Italian poets.

A Way into the Canticle

Formal imagination needs the idea of composition. Material imagination needs the idea of combination. [2]

These words of the philosopher, Gaston Bachelard, are essential to understanding "The Canticle of the Creatures." We usually think of a poem as an object attentively made, built of carefully crafted images. But "The Canticle of the Creatures" is not the product of such "formal imagination." It is a spontaneous outpouring whose unity and beauty depend upon an imagination that has lived intimately with the elements of earth, water, air, and fire and has dreamed them at a deep level. When the material imagination begins to praise God, it finds these archetypal images rising in new combinations.

Earth, water, air, and fire are the focuses of the deep psychic energy through which Francis praises God. Their combinations are not the usual arrangement of heaviest to lightest element: earth, water, air, and fire. The combinations St. Francis used are original and reveal a soul that profoundly reconciled the masculine and feminine sides of his personality. He paired the elements according to gender, male with female: Brother Fire and Sister Water; Brother Wind and Sister Earth. In addition, the combinations indicate that Francis embraced all of creation as his brother and sister.

All of this leads the Franciscan, Eloi Leclerc, to a wholly new way of reading the Canticle. For Leclerc, the Canticle is a spontaneous poem that maps St. Francis' unconscious. It reveals his soul's integration not only with the world around him, but within its own geography. It is a poem of the cosmos and of the psyche, a poem of the soul's journey into God through spiritual integration.

In his book, *The Canticle of the Creatures: Symbols of Union*, Leclerc looks carefully at the images and the structure of the poem and discovers that the four elements are uniquely defined not only in their choice and combinations, but in the adjectives Francis uses to describe them. Why is fire "handsome and merry," unless it symbolizes something beyond itself?

Leclerc's reading of the Canticle opens a way of meditating in depth on St. Francis' path to God. It illumines the order and symmetry of the poem as the symmetry of an ordered soul: the order, that of the unique combination of the elements; the symmetry, that of the choice of the four primary elements to represent all of creation.

Reading the Canticle as a poem of St. Francis' soul, rather than a poem describing nature, reveals that St. Francis did not simply view nature from a comfortable distance. Rather, he lived in intimate communion with the natural world in all *its* moods and seasons. Nature was the book where he read God's providence and presence, the metaphor of his own soul in *its* moods and seasons. It is not surprising, then, that when he sang the song that summarized his whole life, the images that rose into his consciousness were images of the natural world.

By the time he sang "The Canticle of the Creatures," St. Francis had allowed the Creator to heal all divisions within him; and he sang of the unity and harmony of all creation. His eyes were incarnational, wholistic; his heart was one with everything that existed.

Adding to the richness of St. Francis' vision, there is a deep significance to the word translated into English as "through." St. Francis praises God through all things. In the medieval Umbrian dialect the word is *per*, one of those rich, untranslatable words every language has. It means through-with-in-for-by means of, so that when Francis praises God *through* Sister Water, he is praising God *through-with-in-for-by* means of water—an extremely rich concept. In a sense, he enters into the element of water and sings, "May you be praised, Lord, *through* this water; may you be praised *for* water which cannot praise you except in us; be praised, Lord, *with* water for we are water and largely came from water, and we are blessed with water, baptized with water." The small word *per*, then, is a kind of shorthand for a profound mediation of material images.

Surely, St. Francis' favorite image was light: the light of Brother Sun and the stars, the reflected light of Sister

Moon, the illuminating/burning light of Brother Fire. Since he was virtually blind when he sang his Canticle, the light St. Francis praised is an internal light rising from his unconscious depths and revealing his deepest desire: to be one with the light, the "Most high, all powerful, good Lord."

This rich Canticle is a spontaneous outpouring of praise. A hidden treasure reveals its value in the adjectives: "precious" and "chaste" water; "jocund" and "robust" fire. The archetypal nature of this treasure is evident from the very beginning. It is not the poor, crucified Jesus who is addressed, the human and divine Jesus that St. Francis loved all his life, but rather the Most High. This indicates a cosmic elevation of the soul, a deep yearning to ascend. The Most High is an image of what is just beyond the soul's reach, but which comes to the soul in Jesus' emptying of himself, taking the form of a slave, becoming obedient even to death upon a cross, and then rising, bringing with him those who long for the Most High.

CHAPTER 5

A Meditation on the Canticle

A Meditation on the Canticle

Someone once said that God's word disturbs the comfortable and comforts the disturbed. There is truth in this, especially when one begins to pray the word of God. The same is true of "The Canticle of the Creatures." It is not just a pious litany of nature's attributes. It calls us to pray the implications of praising God by means of God's creation. Therefore, as a prayer the poem both challenges and consoles.

What does it mean to pray a poem? It means first of all to enter into an attitude of prayer by slowing down, becoming quiet, opening one's heart to whatever God will say through the words of the poem. It means being attentive to the words themselves, their richness, their surprising twists and turns, their unusual and unconventional meanings and overtones in the hands of the true poet.

To pray a poem implies humility before a work whose architecture may be daunting at first. Trying to understand the complex structure of a poem as an essential part of its meaning makes one humble and receptive to all of creation. The discipline of trying to hear and see the beauty of a poem prepares one to persevere in the discipline of prayer, which, in turn, enables one to truly hear and see the immense creation of God, to notice connections in the world that one never noticed before. The Divine architecture of the universe slowly unfolds, filling one with wonder before the Creator of such a masterpiece. Both in art and in nature one is moved to awe before the created thing and the mind and heart that created it—and awe is the prelude to admiration or adoration. One admires the human artist; one adores the Divine Artist. And from adoration flows all prayer.

St. Francis' poem invites us to look prayerfully at God and his creation. Like God, nature keeps giving itself to us. It yields food and water and beautiful flowers; it gives shade and sunlight, changing seasons and temperatures. Yet we seldom give back or even try to protect this enormous source of fruitfulness. Nature endures, but our lack of reverence, our wastefulness, is beginning to take its toll on even so generous a benefactor.

St. Francis calls us to a renewed attentiveness and reverence, to see that all created things are our brothers and sisters, that we are all interdependent. Most importantly, St. Francis reminds us of the source of this vast interrelated family: God the Creator.

> **Most High, all-powerful, good Lord,**
> **yours is the praise,**
> **the glory and the honor**
> **and every blessing.**
> **They belong to you alone, Most High,**
> **and no one is worthy**
> **to speak your name.**

St. Francis begins his Canticle with words similar to those he uttered before the crucifix of San Damiano at the very beginning of his life in God: "Most High glorious God." After over twenty years praising and loving God, Francis now expands his address. By naming the Most High as the source of all goodness, honor, and blessing, he is invoking "the mystical name of the Triune God whose image is impressed on all creation and who is known only by one who has been crucified with Christ".[1]

Most High, all-powerful. God is the height, the summit of all that is. For St. Francis the way to this height is through a descent, a humbling of oneself, a falling into the earth and dying like a seed, a reaching down to those who have fallen by the wayside, like the lepers who lived on the swamp-like plain below the spur of Mount Subasio.

St. Francis' willingness to descend to work with the lepers enabled him to ascend the mountain of La Verna where he received, in a profound mystical experience, the sacred stigmata.

Like *Most High*, the adjective *all-powerful* indicates a paradox, for it is the all-powerful God who hangs powerless on the cross. Through surrender, the crucified Christ becomes the resurrected, all-powerful Christ. Even here is found paradox, because the power of the resurrected Christ is the power of love, not the power that lords it over others and imposes rule by violence.

Good Lord. Like Jesus before him, St. Francis proclaims God alone as good. The Umbrian people called St. Francis good because he radiated compassion and love for them, for animals and plants, rocks and rivers, stars and moon. However, St. Francis realized that the goodness attributed to human beings is but a reflected gift of the One Lord who alone is good.

St. Francis uses the word "Lord" for God because he has experienced God's sovereignty over him. As a young man, he thought he was lord of his own life and he admired human lords who exercised power over others, who routed evil-doers by force of arms and the glory of battle. Then the true Lord of the universe turned St. Francis' world upside down by telling him to leave knighthood and the field of battle for poverty and the glory of the cross. All of this happened because St. Francis was willing to listen to God's voice, to enter the caves on Mount Subasio to pray in silence and solitude for God's will to be revealed to him. He submitted to a Lord not of this world.

The word "Lord" derives from an Old English word meaning *the keeper of the bread*. Who but God is the ultimate bread-giver, the one who in the Eucharist becomes the Bread of Life? For St. Francis God is the great almsgiver of spiritual as well as material gifts; anything we think we own is really a gift of this Almsgiver, given for our use and not for our possession.

Here, it is important to recall St. Francis' Christocentric spirituality. For him, the Lord is Christ, as described in St. Paul's words, "And God has put all things under his feet and has made him the head over all things for the church, which is his body, the fullness of him who fills all in all" (Eph 1:22–23). The ineffable One, the One whose name we do not know, is made visible in Christ, who "is the image of the invisible God" (Col 1:15).

St. Francis would have celebrated these Pauline passages when he uttered the word, "Lord," for he said, "It is good to read the testimony of the Scriptures, and it is good to seek out the Lord our God in them. But as for me, I have already made so much of Sacred Scripture my own that I have more than enough for my meditation and reflection. I have need of nothing more. I know Christ, the poor crucified one".[2]

> **yours is the praise,**
> **the glory and the honor**
> **and every blessing.**

The very first movement of the poem redirects to God every praise that may have been neglected or focused elsewhere. Its movement is that of the "Our Father," which asserts at the very beginning, "Hallowed be thy name." All prayer—and this poem *is* a prayer—finds its model in the "Our Father"; it begins with praise.

The scientist and naturalist, Edward Armstrong, indicates the union of St. Francis' praise of God with his union with nature. Francis sang, he says,

> not to charm Creation, but because he was charmed by it. Worship being the highest expression of wonder

and reverence, man's lowlier brethren might not be able to offer such explicit, heartfelt, and understanding adoration; but they could join with him according to their several sensibilities and endowments in reverence and praise. The Little Poor Man loosed the tongues of rocks and meadows to raise their voices in brotherly concord singing, "Glory to God in the Highest and on earth peace."[3]

There is a story from an early Franciscan source, *Mirror of Perfection*, that illustrates how Francis' intention in composing the Canticle was to give praise to God.

St. Francis one day said to his companions, "If an emperor were to give his entire kingdom to one of his servants, wouldn't that servant be filled with joy? And if, in addition, he gave him his whole empire, wouldn't the servant be even happier?" And he continued, "Then I too should rejoice in my infirmities and troubles, take comfort in the Lord, and give thanks always to God the Father, and to his only Son, our Lord Jesus Christ, and to the Holy Spirit for the great grace they've given me: namely, to know for certain, even while I am still clothed in the flesh, that I am assured of the kingdom, I an unworthy servant.

"So, for God's praise, for our consolation, and for the edification of others, I want to compose a new

*Francis receives the wounds of the Lord
on Mount La Verna (Tuscany) in 1224*

song, a canticle to the Lord through his creatures, whom we use every day, and without whom we cannot live and through whom the human race greatly offends its Creator. We are constantly ungrateful for his gifts and blessings, and we do not praise the Lord, Creator, Giver of all good gifts, as we should."

Then he sat down and began to meditate for a while. And afterward he began to sing, "Most High, all-powerful, good Lord, etc.," and he taught his companions the words and the melody.[4]

Glory. "We were there when he was given honor and glory by God the Father, when the voice came to him from the Supreme Glory, saying, 'This is my Son, my Beloved, with whom I am well pleased'" (2 Pt 1:17). What is glory? And why does Francis choose glory as the second attribute that belongs to God alone? As reflected in the Second Letter of Peter, the glory of God is the majesty and splendor attendant upon a manifestation of God; it is also the honor of God, God's resplendent beauty, so appreciated by Francis. What further overtone may be contained in Francis' use of the term, *Glory?* Given the trajectory of Francis' whole life, there is a passage from St. Andrew of Crete that speaks pointedly to *glory,* as Francis would use it.

For sure, [the glory of the Lord] is the cross on which Christ was glorified, Christ the brightness of the Father's glory, as he himself said when he came to his passion: "Now is the Son of man glorified, and in him God is glorified and God will glorify him at once," meaning here by "glory" his being lifted up on the cross. The glory of Christ is the cross and his being lifted up, for he says: "And I, when I am lifted up, will draw all men to myself."[5]

For Christians the cross is at the center of the world, and every Christian, at some point in life, has to come to grips with the mystery of the cross. To enter into prayer is to enter into the truth about Jesus Christ, which can never be severed from his death on a cross and his resurrection. And there is the glory: that death, and all the small deaths in our lives, are but a prelude to resurrection in Christ.

How, then, does prayer prepare us for our own death and resurrection? When we pray, we surrender our own need to control, to hold on. We surrender to the working of God's Holy Spirit within us. We acknowledge that everything is gift, is grace. We cannot force God to speak or to be a felt presence. We can only be totally open to whatever God sends, whether a word of consolation or total silence.

In prayer we wait for God, we trust even though we might be feeling the absence of God, a darkness like the tomb. And then, in time, if we persevere, there is an opening of the tomb, a ray of light, and we know that something like resurrection has happened to us. This is the dynamic of the cross and resurrection, the dynamic of that daily dying we call prayer.

Every Blessing. God is blessing, and only God can bless or sanctify; and all blessing comes from God. St. Francis learned already as a young man that what God blesses leads to life and what is not blessed by God is death-dealing, brings sadness and loss of purpose. His experience of war and prison were constant reminders to him of what life was like outside God's blessing when he had been seeking fame and power, and not God's will. Once he found how blessed the poor in spirit are, especially the lepers he encountered, he knew that true blessing abides where the poor Christ is most visible in God's creatures.

One can know such blessing through prayer. Prayer invites us to enter into God's perspective as revealed in Sacred Scripture. To pray is like seeing with God's eyes that look and see what we don't see: blessed are the poor in spirit, the meek, the pure of heart, the persecuted. In prayer we meet the God who sees as blessed those we either reject or avoid. Lord, teach us to pray with your heart, to see with your eyes.

**And no one is worthy
to speak your name.**

To name something is to know who or what it is. Therefore, to name God is to somehow possess God or have power over him. We use the word "God," but God's real name is hidden in mystery. Jesus addresses God as "Abba, Father," but that epithet describes God's generative activity and Providence, not the hidden name that no one is worthy to speak. Moses knew God only as "I am who am," which is again descriptive, a phrase that hides God within God's essence. The Greek word *kyrios*, the Latin word *Dominus*, the Hebrew word *Adonai*, and the English word *Lord* all represent the ineffable name Yhwh.

So "other" is God that no one knows God except the Son and those to whom it is given to know. In other words (and St. Francis was deeply aware of this), whatever we know of God is gift. No one is worthy to merit such knowledge; and even those to whom God has been revealed do not know God's name.

Praised be you, my Lord, with all your
creatures,
especially Sir Brother Sun,
who makes the day and enlightens us through
you.
And he is lovely, shining with great splendor
for he heralds, you, Most High.

Praised be you, my Lord, with all your creatures.
How beautifully the Italian juxtaposes *Signore*, with all its
big, open vowels, with the small vowels in *cum tucte le tue*.
God the big vowel, we the small. It's as if the English translation for creatures should be all your *itsy bitsy little ones*.

St. Francis is able to praise God *with* all God's creatures because he is small like them, because he has embraced them all, and in so doing has embraced the totality
of his own soul. When Francis was reconciled with all of
creation, he was reconciled with everything within as well.
This is the dynamic that figured in Francis' reconciliation
with the wolf who terrorized the citizens of Gubbio:

As soon as he had heard the news of the wolf of
Gubbio, Francis felt sympathy for the wolf. There was
something of the wolf in all of nature, that ravenous
hunger, that restless pursuit, that baring of the fangs,

so symbolic of what is wild and violent in all of us. But he saw in the wolf not so much the stalker as the stalked. Everyone feared wolves and disliked them, and he saw in the eyes of wolves a fear, a hunted look, an anger and hostility that wanted to devour everything in sight in order to avenge their own hurt and alienation. Wolves, after all, were like people. If you feared them and ostracized them and excluded them, they eventually turned into what you were afraid they were anyway.[6]

St. Francis is a mystic of the Incarnation. For him union with God is not outside and above nature, but within it. As in the Virgin Mary, the Holy Spirit descends into the womb of humanity and from that Divine impregnation, God is born *in* us and *among* us. St. Francis focused on God's entrance into human history, rather than emphasizing the ascent toward heaven: it is not what we do to ascend to God that is important, but what God does in descending to us and how we respond to this Divine initiative. One waits in anticipation of the indwelling of God in such a creation-centered spirituality. Yet, the waiting is not passive; it involves active interaction with all of creation by doing the will of God. As St. Francis himself wrote in his "Letter to All the Faithful" in the year 1220: "We are his spouses when our faithful souls are wed to Jesus Christ by the Holy Spirit. We are his brothers and sisters when we do the will of his Father who is in heaven."

It is important to point out that these two movements, one of our "ascent" and the other of God's "descent," are not necessarily contradictory. St. Teresa of Avila combined the two practically when she said that we should work as if everything depended on us and pray as if everything depended on God. Furthermore, these movements are paradoxical: God's coming down is our going up, and our going up involves descending first into creation, just as Jesus Christ did when he came among us as a human being and entered into communion with creation.

The emphasis of each kind of spirituality is different. One may endeavor to slough off human creatureliness in order to ascend to God, while another strives to meet God within human nature and the realm of creation, but they have in common human work and Divine gift. In the end, what is important is union with God. How one experiences such union will depend on how one sets out to meet God.

St. Francis' experience is clear: he sees Christ everywhere; it is through and with Christ in all of creation that Francis praises the Most High God; and it is this same Christ who works in us and through us. Our work is to become brothers and sisters to all creatures; our prayer is praise and gratitude for their and our creation, redemption, and sanctification. For St. Francis, to be in a brotherly/sisterly relationship with creatures precludes domination and possession. Creatures are gifts of the Most High, as so many of the early Franciscan stories celebrate.

The story of St. Francis and the pheasant is only one of many that relates the trust and rapport the saint of Assisi had with animals. He was a brother to them, as to all creation, rather than someone to be feared:

> Once when St. Francis was ill, a nobleman sent him a live pheasant which he had recently caught. And as soon as the pheasant saw St. Francis, it went to his side and would not be separated from him. Many times the brothers set the pheasant outside so that it could go free, but it always came back to St. Francis. Finally, the brothers gave the pheasant to a visitor. But when the man brought the pheasant home, it would not eat. He then returned the pheasant to the brothers, and as soon as the pheasant saw St. Francis, it went to him and began to eat heartily.[7]

Especially Sir Brother Sun. Again the Italian vowels open up, revealing Brother Sun as the image of the Most High, all-powerful, good Lord, who *makes the day and enlightens us through you.* At the time of St. Francis, the earth was believed to be the center of the universe, and the sun was one of the six planets that circled the earth and gave it light and life. The sun, therefore, was an apt symbol for God, the ultimate source of our light and life.

Like God, the sun continues to give light and energy; it is not consumed. That is why St. Francis first addresses Brother Sun, the symbol of God the Creator of life.

To take for granted something so obvious as the sun, to lose reverence for its centrality in our life, is akin to what we can do to our relationship with God. God, of course, continues to create independently of our attention and does not need us in order to be God. But something happens to us when we fail to be grateful. We make gods of ourselves and begin not only to wound the world around us, but to shrink in vision, consciousness, and love. Gratitude, on the other hand, expands the soul from its small self-preoccupation to praise.

To recall ourselves to gratitude, we can do something as simple as taking the time to look at the horizon, at nature. Looking is the beginning of really seeing; when

*Scene depicting the death of Francis,
the "Little Poor Man" of Assisi on October 3, 1226*

we finally see, we appreciate; and when we appreciate, we know how to respond.

And he is lovely, shining with great splendor for he heralds you, Most High.

In this line we see the way St. Francis prayed by means of creatures. Brother Sun is an image, a "herald" of the Most High. For St. Francis, prayer is basically opening up the mind and heart to God. No words are necessary; only receptivity is required, like one standing open-armed, face lifted to the sun. But in trying to make so seemingly simple a gesture of turning to God, one ends up turning his or her whole life around. St. Francis' turning toward the Most High God involved a lifetime of turning his life around in order to end up facing God—and this is prayer.

The Canticle shows us a map of how St. Francis became this kind of living prayer. He did not turn away from creatures; he became one with them in a fraternal relationship that resisted domination. In that relinquishment of possession, all creatures pointed to God as their origin and destiny. As St. Bonaventure wrote so succinctly in his *Major Life of St. Francis:* "He delighted in all the works of God's hands and from a joyful, earthly vision his mind soared heavenward to the life-giving source and cause of everything.[8]

> **Praised be you, my Lord, through Sister Moon and Stars.**
> **You have formed them in heaven, lightsome and precious and fair.**

In St. Francis' day, the Church identified the sun with Christ and the moon with Mary, who receives the light of Christ and reflects this light to us even at night when we no longer see the sun. Mary, like the Church herself, is filled with God's light, and through her mediation sheds that light on us. St. Francis' connection of the moon and Mary, the stars and the feminine, is consonant with the theological speculations of his time.

Innocent III, the pope who approved St. Francis' Rule, taught that when we are in sin, the sun is hidden, but the moon is still on the horizon. It is to Mary, God's mother and our mother, that we should turn. And so it was that St. Francis made Mary the Patroness of the Franciscan Order and turned to her for her intercession. He named the small chapel that is the cradle of the Order after Mary, Our Lady of the Angels.

When St. Francis sings of the moon, he sings of the feminine and, in particular, of Mary who is, in his words, "Virgin become Church." Mary is the virgin mother who like the Church brings forth God into the world. She is "lightsome and precious and fair." In the Middle Ages what was said of Mary was said of the Church as well; both had been impregnated by the Holy Spirit and were thereby mothers of the Mystical Body: Mary gave birth to Christ, the head, and the Church gave birth to the members of Christ, the Body.

Mary continues to be that mediating presence today. We turn to her in prayer; we find images of her in our own age, especially as she has appeared to us in modern times as Our Lady of the Immaculate Conception, the healing mother of Lourdes, the woman surrounded by stars and standing on the moon of Guadalupe, the mother of conversion at Fatima.

The first adjective Francis uses for Sister Moon and Stars is "clarite," a word which Francis coins meaning clear, full of light, but also resonant of the name of Clare. This closeness, indicative of Francis' acceptance of the feminine, is illustrated in this popular Franciscan legend:

> It happened once that St. Francis and Brother Leo went to Siena together, and St. Francis was sad because

the people had shown them so little courtesy. He began to think of his dear Assisi where he had his spiritual sons and of his beloved daughter in God, St. Clare. He knew how much Clare was suffering because of her devotion to holy poverty, and he feared that she might become ill. Weighed down by these thoughts, he felt he couldn't walk any further once he and his companion got to the place where the road turns into the hill country. He dragged himself to a well and for a long time just stood looking down into the clear water. Then he lifted his head and said joyfully to Brother Leo:

"Brother Leo, little lamb of God, what do you think I've been looking at in the water of the well?"

"The moon that is reflected there," replied Brother Leo.

"No, Brother Leo, not Sister Moon, but, through the Lord's mercy, I've been looking at the true face of our sister, Lady Clare. Her countenance is so pure and full of holy joy that all my fears are gone. I know now that she has been given that perfect joy which God gives his dear ones by pouring upon them the treasures of holy poverty."[9]

St. Francis speaks with ease of the feminine in this story and in the Canticle. This ease was not always the case however. During the early years following his conversion, Francis often gave evidence of being anything but comfortable with women. He was fearful of women, seeing them, as medieval theology taught, either as seductresses and temptresses, or as unattainable, idealized creatures like the Virgin Mary. But he grew past this discomfort, as well as with his initial discomfort with his own feminine side.

There is a famous dream that Francis related to Pope Innocent III at the time he requested approval of his way of life. It illustrates how comfortable Francis was, even then, with the feminine side of his person:

> In order to determine if this new way of life was truly God's will and not Francis' own, the Pope told Francis to go away and pray further about his request to live Gospel poverty. When he returned the next day, Francis told the Pope of a dream he had that night.
>
> "Holy Father, there was a beautiful woman who lived in the desert. And one day when the king was passing, he saw the woman and was smitten by her beauty. He wanted her to have his children, so he had a marriage document drawn up, and he married the woman of the desert.

"She had many sons by him; and when they grew up, she told them they need have no fear of want, for they were the sons of the King, and he would give them everything they needed. And so when they arrived one day at court, the King recognized his likeness in them. 'Whose sons are you?' he asked. 'We are the children of the woman of the desert.'

"The King immediately acknowledged them as his own and embraced them saying, 'So many strangers sit at my table and eat; how much more so should you.'

"He then ordered that these children of his be summoned to his court and there be provided for.

Then Francis said to the Pope, who questioned how Francis and his Brothers would survive if they lived as beggars without anything of their own, "Holy Father, I am the poor woman of the desert, and God is the King. He has had mercy on me and through me he has begotten legitimate children."[10]

How naturally St. Francis speaks about himself as "mother." Looking at the masculine/feminine dimensions of the Canticle and of St. Francis' person, illustrates the sort of man St. Francis was. We bring to prayer who we are: a warrior prays like a warrior; a timid person prays with timidity; an integrated person prays out of her or his integration; and a broken person, out of brokenness.

To see such an integration of polarities within St. Francis, within his Canticle, and within the universe itself gives us courage to walk our own way of the cross, to let go of things that are possessing us, to embrace those fallen by the wayside of our society, of our times. Such a passage cannot be made without prayer, for interior prayer is a rehearsal for the life we live outside of formal prayer, the charity for which all prayer prepares us.

Because the integration of the self involves an acceptance of both the masculine and the feminine and learning to reconcile them, the following stanzas on wind and water, the male and female dimensions of generativity, express something of how profound was Francis' personal integration toward the end of his life.

> **Praised be you, my Lord, through Brother Wind,**
> **through air and cloud,**
> **and calm and every weather**
> **through which you sustain your creatures.**

The surprising words of this stanza of Brother Wind are: "and calm and every weather / through which you sustain your creatures." Every weather? Does that include storms and hurricanes, drought and cyclones, floods and blizzards? Or does the poet mean only that weather which sustains God's creatures? Perhaps both interpretations are possible, since God's love sustains us in all weather, even in that which is seemingly destructive.

This ambiguity is interesting, especially when expanded to include the union of wind and water as seen in Genesis when, in the beginning, the world was covered with water and the breath of God blew over the waters like a wind, bringing forth life. This is the same breath Jesus exhales in his last moment on the cross; blood and water issue from his side, and the Church is born—another association of breath with new life. To reconcile within oneself wind and water is to embrace the generative power of God's Spirit breathing life out of the vast waters of the soul, whether those waters be turbulent or calm.

> **Praised be you, my Lord, through Sister Water,**
> **so very useful and humble**
> **and precious and chaste.**

Sacred Scripture is replete with water imagery, from the Genesis passage previously mentioned, to Psalm 23 in which the psalmist prays to the Lord who "leads me beside still waters," to Jesus addressing the Samaritan woman at the well with the words, "those who drink of the water that I will give them will never be thirsty. The water that I will give will become in them a spring of water gushing up to eternal life" (Jn 4:14); to the Book of Revelation in which John writes, "Then the angel showed me the river of the water of life, bright as crystal, flowing from the throne of God and of the Lamb through the middle of the street of the city" (Rev 22:1–2a).

St. Francis sees in water a sister of fountains and quiet running streams, the lake of contemplation rather than the violence of stormy seas. The very rhythm of the Italian—*e multo utile et humile / et pretiosa et casta*—echoes the sound of slow, dripping water.

Surely St. Francis, a man who lived much of his life out of doors, was accustomed to many forms of water. He walked in the rain, bathed in the streams of Umbria, looked into the depths of Lake Trasimeno, drank from mountain streams where La Verna rose from the Tuscan landscape. Water was indeed useful and humble and precious and chaste: useful in its cleansing and slaking of thirst; humble in asking nothing of us and giving so much. Water is purification and immersion; water is the pre-

St. Francis in the glory of heaven

cious depths we enter along with Christ in order to emerge reborn in him; water is as chaste as the innocent beings that issued from its depths in the beginning of Creation.

> **Praised be you, my Lord, through Brother**
> **Fire,**
> **through whom you illumine our night.**
> **And he is handsome and merry,**
> **robust and strong.**

When St. Francis calls fire his brother, he is speaking about more than the flames that dart about in a bonfire. As Leclerc points out, fire is a dynamic image that moves St. Francis to praise. Fire is never just an external reality for human beings. It awakens profound resonances of desire, love, hate, of the need to be attached. Fire is a force that is both consoling and consuming. As such, it is one of the great symbols of the ardent energies of life, from the noblest spiritual action to the wildest, most primitive passion. For the ancient Greeks, the god who speaks in fire is a life-giving force that seeks union, communication, and self-propagation. This living fire that seeks to fuse all things into oneness is what the Greeks named Eros, the power to love, the active energy of the soul. Therefore, one whose imagination communes in an intense and cosmic way with fire is dealing with Eros, the primordial affective power of the soul, as is illustrated in early Franciscan stories.

The Meal with St. Clare

St. Francis had the table readied on the bare ground, as was his custom. And when it was time to eat, St. Francis and St. Clare sat down together with one of his companions and one of St. Clare's companions around the humble table where his other companions were gathered. But at the first course St. Francis began to speak about God in so holy and profound and divine and marvelous a way that he and St. Clare and her companion and all the others who were at that poor little table were rapt in God by the overabundance of divine grace that descended upon them.

And while they were sitting there, in a rapture, with their eyes and hands raised to heaven, the people of Assisi and Bettona and the entire district thought that the Church of St. Mary of the Angels and everything around it, including the forest, was aflame with an immense fire. The men of Assisi ran down there to save the Place and put out the fire, because they were convinced that everything was burning up.

But when they reached the Place, they saw that nothing was on fire. Entering the Place, they found St. Francis with St. Clare and all the companions sitting around that very humble table, rapt in the contemplation of God and invested with power from on high.

Then they understood that it had been a heavenly and not a material fire that God had miraculously shown them to symbolize the fire of divine love burning in the souls of those holy friars and nuns.[11]

The Fiery Chariot

And behold, about midnight, when some of the brothers were resting and some were praying in silence with great devotion, a most splendid fiery chariot entered through the door of the house and circled the room two or three times; a huge globe of light rested above it, much like the sun, and it lit up the night. The watchers were dazed, and those who had been asleep were frightened; and they felt no less a lighting up of the heart than a lighting up of the body. Drawing together, they began to ask one another what it was since by the strength and grace of that great light each one's conscience was revealed to the others.

Finally they understood and knew it was the soul of their holy father that was shining with such brilliance.[12]

Thus, for Francis, the image of fire is both an external reality and a symbol of a profound interior reconciliation. The fire that has become his brother symbolizes a fire that has been transformed from a blind power of chaotic passion to a life-giving force; from a force that burns to a force that warms and enlightens. Transformed fire is passion transformed by charity.

> **Praised be you, my Lord, through our Sister,**
> **Mother Earth.**
> **In her sovereignty she nourishes us,**
> **bringing forth all kinds of fruits**
> **and colored flowers and herbs.**

How separated we have grown from the earth! Most of us let others grow and process our food and don't feel particularly connected to the source of our nourishment. Do we have a plot of ground to cultivate, even if only in the form of a potted plant? We are busy pursuing money, fame, power, knowledge, even spiritual sustenance, etc., and on our way we pass by the earth's vegetation and animal life, the contemplation of which could nourish our souls.

Pilgrims come to Assisi to find St. Francis and sometimes take little or no notice of the finches, skylarks, crows, robins, starlings, bobolinks, and sparrows. Nor do they notice the cyclamen, blackberry, ginestra, cypress, oak, fir, pine, and poplar on Mount Subasio, where St. Francis spent so much time in prayer and contemplation. Nor do they ask what animals, if any, still inhabit the diminished forest of Mount Subasio. Are there still wild boars there, or wolves, as in St. Francis' time?

How deeply we need St. Francis' vision to counteract the destruction the modern age is wreaking on creation. How cruelly we have bombed Sister Earth, and so hurriedly stripped her of trees that more than an acre of rain forest is lost every second! Flowers appear on our tables from countries where those who plant and water and harvest them are paid less than the minimum wage; though surrounded by beauty, they live in impoverished, desperate conditions. In Francis' vision, the earth is a realm that, when respected and reverenced, continues "bringing forth all kinds of fruits / and colored flowers and herbs." There is a charming story told by St. Francis' early companions, Leo, Ruffino, and Angelo, that goes like this:

> One day, Francis told the brother gardener not to plant the whole garden with food, but to set aside a plot for those plants which in their season would bloom with Brother Flowers. He said the reason the brother gardener should plant this pretty little flower bed with its sweetly scented herbs and flowering plants was because it would invite all who saw it to praise God; for every creature says, "God made me for you, oh human!"[13]

Granted, St. Francis lived at a time when people were still close to the earth as *the* source of life. Everything depended on the earth and the people's working with the earth to ensure a sufficient yield of crops. Our modern separation from the earth may make it harder for us to grasp Francis' images or, more particularly, those of Sacred Scripture, which relate so intimately to nature and to the nature of the soul's relationship with God. Images, for example, of sheep and the shepherd, the vine and the branches, the seed that falls into the ground and dies, the mustard seed, streams and wells, etc., may be foreign to us. Yet, God has chosen those images to symbolize the relationship between God and creatures. They feed our inner life and also move us to reverence the earth.

Jesus tells us pointedly in the parable of the sheep and goats that we will be judged by what we did not do:

> For I was hungry and you gave me no food. I was thirsty and you gave me nothing to drink. I was a stranger and you did not welcome me, naked and you did not give me clothing, sick and in prison and you did not visit me (Mt 25:42–44).

Perhaps we can add, "And when my Creation cried out to you for stewardship and reverence, you did nothing"?

St. Francis saw all of creation as a sacrament of God's provident love. He praised God with and through creation, and respected her sovereign rights. If that sounds naïve to us today, then all the more do we need to hear St. Francis' words. There is a need for his prophetic language. And this, too, is a part of prayer: to be willing to listen to the truth of our human situation. Otherwise, prayer is "pollyanna-like," and we become sheep following shepherds other than Christ.

> **Praised be you, my Lord,**
> **for those who forgive**
> **in your love**

and who bear sickness
and trial.

One of the deepest effects of forgiveness is that it enables us to let go of the past and its hurts. When we cannot forgive, we do not live *in* the present or *for* the future; we wallow in the past. We allow resentment and hurts, either real or imaginary, to affect the rhythm of our lives so that we are not free to live in the moment and fulfill present possibilities for growth and joy.

Francis had personally experienced how difficult forgiveness can be. When he renounced his own father, claiming that God was his true father, Pietro was angry and saddened. There is no indication that any reconciliation between them ever occurred. Some believe that the description of the unrepentant dying man in Francis' "Letter to All the Faithful" was motivated by his own father's death, making this stanza on forgiveness all the more poignant.

The power in these words of the poem comes from the deep inner reconciliation that the poet must have reached within himself. St. Francis must have forgiven the betrayal he felt when some of his Brothers were not embracing Lady Poverty, but living comfortable lives. He must have forgiven his illnesses; forgiven himself for not following Christ as perfectly as he wanted to; forgiven the Church for the abuses he no doubt saw in some of its members and leaders. In short, Francis must have had to forgive life itself for being unfair and hard at times.

This forgiveness was not easy for St. Francis; he knew it could only be done in and through God, as he wrote in his paraphrase of the Our Father:

> "As we forgive those who trespass against us," and what we do not fully forgive, do you, O Lord, make us fully forgive, so that for your sake we may truly love our enemies and devoutly intercede for them with you, thereby rendering no evil for evil, but striving in you to do good to all.[14]

Out of this forgiveness comes:

> **Blessed are those who endure in peace,**
> **by you, Most High,**
> **they will be crowned.**

Our endurance in peace is a participation in and identification with the suffering and passion of Christ. Forgiveness conforms us to Christ who, through his own patient endurance, is crowned King of the Universe. It is

*Allegory on Francis united in a lifelong relationship
to his mystical bride "Lady Poverty"*

Christ who in turn crowns us, because we are now conformed to him. In a way, forgiveness enables us to be sovereigns of our own lives because it frees us to live as God's children.

The growth of a forgiving heart enables us to endure in peace the trials of life. Instead of becoming bitter, the forgiving person becomes an instrument of peace, absorbing attack and insult as a step toward reconciliation. For St. Francis, to forgive was to be united with Christ.

Sickness, too, can make us bitter and angry, which in turn only worsens what is already perceived as intolerable. But to endure in peace, to forgive even one's own frailty and life's unfairness, transforms the heart, and the transformed heart radiates peace to others, even in the face of conflict, hatred, and illness.

Praised be you, my Lord, through our Sister Bodily Death from whom no living being can escape.

How many smaller, symbolic "dyings" St. Francis must have embraced through his practice of asceticism to be able to welcome bodily death as his sister! The reign of God is so established within him that bodily death is no longer feared. He *knows* that he is already in God's kingdom; it dwells within him. Though what is seriously sinful has been put to death in Francis, the emphasis is not on the Manichaean idea of what *Francis* has done to remove sin from his life, but rather on what *God* has done in him. Asceticism is not an end in itself or a punishing of the body in a kind of spiritualized masochism. Rather, it is a way of guarding God's kingdom within, which is also an external kingdom whose King is Christ the Lord. Francis embraces the work of God in him, for sin can no longer reign where God has set up his throne.

Should there be any lingering suspicion that the Canticle is not a poem of cosmic and psychic integration, but only a romantic praise of creatures, the final stanza on death dispels such doubt. So great is St. Francis' poverty and his reconciliation of the opposing forces within, that he greets death—not just the idea of death, but his own existential death—as his sister. Thomas of Celano writes:

> Francis spent the remaining few days before his death in praise, teaching his much-beloved companions to praise Christ with him. He also asked all creatures to praise God and, using the words he'd composed earlier, exhorted them to love God. He even exhorted death itself, terrible and hated by all, to give praise; and

joyfully going to meet it, he invited death to be his lodger. "Welcome," he said, "my Sister Death."[15]

How dreadful for those who die in mortal sin!

So deep was the intimacy between St. Francis and God that even the thought of sin was abhorrent to him. Because St. Francis knew God so deeply in prayer, his greatest fear was to be separated from the love of his life. Death itself could not sever that relationship; in fact, death was the passage to an even deeper intimacy with and vision of the Beloved. Only sin could separate him from God. Only sin was real death.

One who does not pray or who has not persevered in prayer cannot know sin as a separation from the Beloved. For it is only in prayer that we come to experience intimacy with God and learn how terrible sin is. When St. Francis says, "How dreadful for those who die / in mortal sin," he feels that dreadfulness; he knows what it means and why sin is so terrible, and why living God's will brings blessedness.

How blessed are those who are found in your most holy will, ...

Contemplation for St. Francis is searching for the will of God in all things. God's face is revealed in God's will, and Francis' apostolic life proceeded out of the contemplation of God's face. It is no wonder, then, that Francis does not use an abstract phrase like, *How blessed are those who are found / in grace.* He is much more concrete:

> **who are found**
> **in your most holy will,**
> **for the second death**
> **can do them no harm.**

The coming of death is inevitable, but not something we usually welcome. However, if we are in God's most holy will, her arrival is really the beginning of eternal life where the second death of unending torment cannot touch us. Sister Death's embrace is the final poverty, the final stripping away of selfishness. And so, as Francis prepares for death, he asks to be stripped of his clothing and laid naked on Sister Earth. Lying on the very earth from which Adam was created, he will be refashioned, transformed into the resurrected person who lives forever in union with God.

Not only human beings, but the other creatures Francis loved, knew that he had been transformed in death, that someone special had entered eternity. In his Treatise on the Miracles, Thomas of Celano wrote of Francis' death:

> The Larks are friends of daylight and shun the shadows of twilight. But on the eve that St. Francis passed from this world to Christ, just as twilight was descending, the larks rose up to the roof of his cell and began circling it with clamor of wing beat and song. No one knew if they were singing with joy or sadness, for their voices were filled with joyful tears and sad joy, as if they were orphaned children weeping and singing their father into heaven. The city guards who were keeping watch there were filled with wonder and they summoned others to witness the sight.[16]

**Praise and bless my Lord,
thank him and serve him
humbly but grandly!**

St. Francis turned the medieval world on its head. As a man whose early ambition and dream was to be a knight, he understood the allure of the quest, of going after the Grail. But something happened somewhere between that dream of knighthood and receiving the wounds of Christ. St. Francis realized that life is not so much the pursuit of an ideal as the uncovering of God's gift already within us.

Out of this recognition of God's bounty in creating, redeeming, and sanctifying us, comes these last three lines of the Canticle. St. Francis remembers; he is grateful; he responds. His response, though humble, is grand after the manner of the knightly spirit he still has within. That paradox of grand humility is characteristic of St. Francis and how he responded to the overwhelming realization that God had accomplished in him everything he ever wanted, even before he knew the gift of God, namely, that he was created in God's image; redeemed by the passion, death, and resurrection of God's only Son; and made holy by the power of God's Spirit. Once he realized this, he only had to uncover and live out the implications of so great a reality. His life became more response than quest, more returning than acquiring gifts, more living out God's reality for him than searching for another of his own making.

The Parable of the Canticle

This whole meditation and all of the Canticle, by way of a summary and conclusion, can be framed as a poetic parable.

What is ordinary, or usual, is dismissed.
A man, for example,
at a time of many crucifixions,
dies on a cross outside of Jerusalem.
He's buried in a friend's tomb.
And that's the end of it,
except that three days later
a woman who loved the man
is talking to the gardener
outside the tomb
and suddenly realizes he is the man.
She tells his friends,
they come to the tomb,
and it is empty,
except for a discarded winding sheet and an angel.

This story changes how we see the world.
Never again will anything be
simply what it seems to be.
And those with eyes to see will see it.
Those who don't see
will believe or not believe
those who do see into the mystery.

People begin to remember
what the crucified man said:
how the bread he blesses
is really his body
and the wine
his blood;
how he and God are one;
how he will rise from the dead;
how his Spirit gives new eyes
to those who will accept that Spirit;
how they who believe in him
will leave behind empty tombs;
how they will all be together forever
somewhere beyond what even eyes
    of the Spirit can see
here where everything seems to die,
where everything seem to be
just what it is to eyes that die.

Nothing historical can give one Spirit-eyes.
What happened is only
what happened as seen with eyes that die.
What is lies beyond

what such eyes can see.
History can only say
something happened;
it cannot give eyes to see what is.

If this, then, be the truth of the man,
what must be the truth of other human beings,
of plants and animals,
rocks and clouds,
sun and moon and stars,
and everything that is!

This is what St. Francis of Assisi sees, what he sings in his "Canticle of the Creatures." This is why he retreated to solitary, silent places. This is what he preached to the birds who listened with their "other ear" to the human who spoke with that "other voice," the voice of the Spirit.

And that is why "The Canticle of the Creatures" is really about Jesus who, dying on a cross, seemed to some to have died an ordinary man. To see who Jesus really is with eyes of the Spirit is to see into the mystery of things. Only one with such eyes can understand what "The Canticle of the Creatures" is all about. St. Francis' Canticle is a concrete expression of the mystery of the Incarnation, the mystery of God's entering the world in the person of Jesus Christ. In that Divine act, all of creation is touched by God. The poet and saint, Francis of Assisi, sees what God's touch has done to every creature and, in the Canticle, he sings of that mystery. Nothing is simply ordinary because of the extraordinary visitation of God. That is the theme, the beginning and end of St. Francis' "The Canticle of the Creatures."

Chapter 6

Ways to Read Poetry Prayerfully

> To write is to descend,
> to excavate, to go underground.

> — *Anais Nin*

1. Begin Journal Writing

An acquaintance of mine, an inveterate diary writer, began keeping what she calls a two-line journal when someone gave her a daybook with room for only two lines of writing each day. The book was too beautiful to discard and too meager of space to use as a traditional journal, so she decided to keep this particular book for two lines of writing based on something she had observed that day. She makes an entry each night before retiring and at the end of the month she reads through her entries—amazed at what she has seen and recorded.

We all would be amazed, I'm sure, if we were to do something similar. And what a relief for most of us to be committed to writing only two lines a day! As with prayer, if we bite off too much at first, we probably won't continue. But the concept of a two-line entry is less daunting and so we manage to continue. And what is modestly, realistically begun, can lead to more ambitious goals, like a longer time of reading or writing or sitting in contemplation. After a while we might settle into a comfortable armchair and spend a longer time thinking about what we saw on a given day before trying to record the experience in two lines. In the same way, much silence and solitude, waiting and surrendering, may be needed before a word rises from within that we recognize as true and honest prayer.

We don't have to record our two lines in rhyme and meter, but we do have to write our two lines each day and let the discipline of doing take us where it will. Similarly, the putting-in of time in the practice of prayer will lead us into an inwardness of fewer and fewer words. One word of prayer, like two lines from a journal, comes at the end of a long process of observations, silence, and solitude. The practice is everything, because putting our thoughts and feelings down on paper or into the computer is what makes the difference between wanting to write and actually writing, just as prayer is praying and not just wanting to pray.

I am convinced that this simple practice of writing and praying a little bit at a time is the best way to appreciate and to pray a poem. It prepares us to approach a poem slowly, carefully, with a new awareness gained from our own practice of trying to pray and to write just two lines every day. "Doing" prepares us for appreciating "the done."

2. Enter the Rooms of the Soul

The word *stanza* in Italian means *room*. Looking at each stanza of a poem as a little room with its own furniture, lighting, and arrangement allows the reader to enter a poem the way he or she would enter a room. Some people enter a room and notice very little. They are so preoccupied with their own thoughts or purposes that they see only what they've come into the room to see. Perhaps we all do this at times. Some people (and all of us at certain times) enter a room as a sanctuary: reverently, slowly, open to whatever is there. That is the way to read a poem, and this kind of reading of a good poem leads naturally into prayer.

Entering the rooms of a poem opens up the rooms of our own souls. The "furniture" of the poem somehow mirrors the "furniture" of our own inner rooms. For example, Shakespeare reminds us of our own experience in this small "room":

> That time of year thou mayst in me behold
> When yellow leaves, or none, or few, do hang
> Upon those boughs which shake against the cold,
> Bare ruined choirs, where late the sweet birds sang.

> —*Sonnet LXXIII*

Who hasn't felt like a barren branch in fall shaking against the cold? We probably would never have thought of the striking metaphor used by Shakespeare, and the images conjure up more than themselves. When do we feel barren? When is the place of our praying like a bare, ruined choir where before there was sweet singing like that of birds? The experience of this small room of a poem makes the reader tremble with recognition. Longing for the return of a time when prayer was like a singing choir, one might cry out, "These things I remember, as I pour out my soul. Why are you cast down my soul? Why are you disquieted within me? Hope in God for I shall again praise him, my help and my God" (Ps 42).

In this, too, is poetry a help to prayer: its images engage the whole person, the emotions as well as the mind.

A poem's images remind us of other "rooms": stanzas from other poems, stanzas from our own experience.

3. Seek the Universal in the Particular

What makes poetry so helpful for prayer is how a poem can be about more than one thing. A poem, for example, can be specifically about the poet's father and yet about many fathers or, as in the case of prayer, about God as Father.

In the poem "Father and Son" by Stanley Kunitz, for example, the poet invokes his dead father:

> At the water's edge, where the smothering ferns
>   lifted
> Their arms, "Father!" I cried, "Return! You know
> The way. I'll wipe the mudstains from your clothes;
> No trace, I promise, will remain. Instruct
> Your son, whirling between two wars,
> In the Gemara of your gentleness,
> For I would be a child to those who mourn
> And brother to the foundlings of the field
> And friend of innocence and all bright eyes.
> O teach me how to work and keep me kind."[1]

Now the irony of the poem is that the poet's father committed suicide when Kunitz was still in his mother's womb. The face the father turns to him in the poem is a terrible revelation: "Among the turtles and the lilies he turned to me / The white ignorant hollow of his face."

The poem is a shattering experience. Reading these lines, one wonders how many have felt this way about their fathers...how many have felt let down and abandoned, even Francis himself? Is the feeling of abandonment a part of growing up? Do we need to know abandonment in prayer in order to move on to love—a love that loves the Other for the Other's sake and not for what we may receive?

The questions suggested by a poem are also the questions of honest prayer. With them the reader begins to turn toward God, invoking God's presence, wondering what God's face will be like. Prayer is not knowledge; prayer is faith and longing for God's presence. And what if God's face is not revealed? Does God speak to me in silence?

Reflecting like this on a poem can lead us into the midst of prayer. We enter into faith, hope, and charity—the very center of prayer. We wait and long for God's face to be revealed. This is how poetry deepens our prayer and keeps it from being sentimental and naïve. Poetry reminds us how much of our lives are mystery. A good poem is honest and invites us to be honest and trust our experience. And honesty persevered in, our faith tells us, will lead us to God.

4. Experience the Power of Metaphor

Here is a little Mary-poem by St. Francis:

Hail, my Lady, Holy Queen, Mary, Mother of God.
You are virgin made church.
You have been chosen in heaven
    by the Most Holy Father.
With his Most Holy Beloved Son
    and the Holy Spirit he has
Consecrated you, so that in you is all fullness
    of grace and every good.
Hail his palace, hail his tabernacle, his house.
Hail his vesture, hail his handmaid, his mother.
And hail all you holy virtues, who through
    the grace and illumination of
The Holy Spirit are poured into the hearts of
Believers, so that you might transform
    unfaithfulness into
Faithfulness to God.[2]

These lines, from St. Francis' "Salutation to the Blessed Virgin Mary," offer some extraordinary insights that lead us to meditation and prayer. He calls Mary, "virgin made church." We might ask, What does that mean? How is Mary the virgin made church? To what depths of theology does that metaphor descend? Only our own meditation can take us there. What is more, those three profound words, *virgin made church*, invite us to study the theology of Mary in order to understand what St. Francis is saying. In so doing we begin to understand the condensation of poetry, how poetry speaks volumes in a few words. Like a crystal the words of a poem have to be studied from different angles; the sun of mind and heart must shine on them if they are to reveal their shimmering truth and beauty.

And what of all the names St. Francis gives Mary: *God's palace, God's tabernacle, house, vesture, handmaid, mother?* How is Mary all of these names? What other names might you give her? Why does St. Francis switch to a praise of all the virtues? Is he still writing of Mary? Are the virtues what make us like Mary? What is Francis saying?

All of these questions remind us that a poem is often a little puzzle requiring that we solve it in order to plumb its mystery. There aren't any easy answers to these questions, because the real answers are revealed in the process of asking the questions, following where they lead us, taking the time to go deeper, to think and feel with the images the poem gives us.

A poem viewed in this way is thinking infused with feeling; and unless we think and feel with the poem, we cannot enter it. Here is a poem in which I invite the reader to think and feel the mystery of Francis' life as metaphor.

ICARUS IN ASSISI

I feel you floating down,
descending from Subasio's crest
like Icarus into his waiting sea.

But you fall towards lepers'
open arms, wolves' hungry jaws.
With them you laugh at the heights

you fell from. Your descent is
ascent to Love who fell
into the Virgin Mary's womb.

Like Christ's, your coming down,
down-coming, rises heavenward.
Poverty's not without wings.

It lifts. And we who live below
rise by going farther down with Him

who fell that we might fly
with poor, bruised hands and feet.

We soar in lepers' skins, we praise
from wolves' and beggars' mouths.[3]

5. Listen to Rhythms and Sounds

A poem has its own music that, like a mantra, re-places the frenetic rhythms of our superficial lives. We enter the rhythm of the poem that could be the rhythm of our own heartbeat, or the movement of the waves of the sea, or of a swinging bell, or a steam engine. For the duration of the poem, we surrender to a rhythm other than the usually erratic rhythm of our daily lives. Listen, for example, to the rhythm of this final couplet from Shakespeare's Sonnet LXXXVIII:

Such is my love, to thee I do belong,
That for thy right myself will bear all wrong.

The strong iambic pentameter beat of these lines pounds home the conviction that the poet will indeed bear all wrong. The beat itself reinforces the poet's de-termination, just as it increases the addressee's convic-tion that yes, the poet will bear all wrong for the lover's right.

Or listen to the repetitive rhythms of the Litany of the Blessed Virgin Mary:

Tower of Ivory, pray for us.
House of Gold, pray for us.
Ark of the Covenant, pray for us.
Morning Star, pray for us.

The insistent beat in these lines emphasizes petition, while at the same time calming the heart.

Sometimes a poem relies, not so much on strong rhythms for effect, as on the repetition of sounds. The Canticle of St. Francis in Italian relies heavily on assonance, the repetition of vowel sounds, as in the repeated "u" sounds in "cum tucte le tue creature" or the "i" and "e" sounds in "Laudato sie, mi signore."

The sounds and rhythms of poetry transport us to another world than the one we are used to in our daily lives. They facilitate listening that is more interior, more attuned to the voice of the soul or of the natural world. They require us to slow down, to read more carefully, paying attention to words and their arrangement on the page, their sound in the ear. All of this can be conducive to the interiority and attentiveness necessary for prayer.

6. Questions that Deepen the Prayerful Reading of a Poem

In picking up a poem to use as prayer, you can ask:

- What does the title of the poem suggest? Does it add to an understanding of the poem?

- In what person is the poem written? First person or third person? And if the poem is in first person, is it the poet speaking, or a "persona" through which the poet is speaking? How does the voice the poem is written in make a difference? For example, does it help you identify with the poem and pray with it?

- What sort of diction does the poem use—e.g. colloquial, formal, etc.? How does this affect your ability to pray with the poem?

- What are the central metaphors of the poem? How do they help you to pray the poem?

- What mood or argument does the poem present? In what way is either or both helpful to your prayer?

- How is the tone of voice compatible with your prayer or meditation?

▨ What parts of the poem resist paraphrase? Is this because they are unclear, or is there mystery here, things said that cannot be said any other way? Are there things in your experience with God that are like that?

▨ What do you find especially beautiful in the poem? How does this beauty call you to prayer, reflection, closer observation of the world around you or within you?

▨ How does this poem draw you into prayer?

7. Read the Poem in Church or a Sacred Place

If you have a favorite poem that leads you into prayer or into the center of your soul, you may want to read the poem in a church or sacred place. It may be a poem written by a saint, for example, and you are even more focused if you are at the saint's shrine or kneeling before her or his statue. The following little poem is one which St. Bernardine of Siena attributed to St. Francis. I find it very moving, especially when I pray the poem before the crucifix that spoke to St. Francis at San Damiano.

May the fiery and honey-sweet
Power of your love, O Lord,

Wean me from all things under
Heaven, so that I may die
For love of your love, you
Who deigned to die
For love of my love.

Find a poem that leads you to prayer and seek out a place that will help you enter into the poem's mystery and deepen your prayer.

8. Read the Poem Aloud

In his book, *How to Read a Poem*, Edward Hirsch says, "Poetry never loses its sense of sacred mystery. Poetry emerged with the chant and the dance. As Sapir puts it, 'Poetry everywhere is inseparable in its origins from the singing voice and the measure of the dance.'"[4] Though we all may not be able to sing well, we can all recite a poem aloud and hear for ourselves the music of the lines, the mesmerizing force of the poem's particular arrangement of words. It is an experience similar to reciting the Psalms aloud rather than reading them silently. There's something mysterious about the sound of the poet's words recited aloud. We hear the words and know their meaning, but we also hear something else that is hard to explain.

In a good poem, the very sound of the line will echo its own meaning. For example, the Alexandrine, or twelve-syllable line with its six strong accents, drags out the line, especially when recited aloud. The English poet Alexander Pope mocks the Alexandrine in this couplet which, when recited aloud, illustrates just how long a line of twelve syllables is:

A needless Alexandrine ends the Song,
That like a wounded Snake, drags its slow length
    along.

A good poem's meaning is reinforced by the very music of its line. The line may be short and curt, like the blows of a boxer who assaults with punches, as in these lines from Thomas Nashe's "A Litany in Time of Plague."

Beauty is but a flower
Which wrinkles will devour;
Brightness falls from the air;
Queens have died young and fair;
Dust hath closed Helen's eye.
I am sick, I must die.
Lord have mercy on us![5]

Or the line may be longer, more meditative, as in these lines from W. B. Yeats's, "Among School Children."

I walk through the long schoolroom questioning;
A kind old nun in a white hood replies;
The children learn to cipher and to sing,
To study reading-books and history,
To cut and sew, be neat in everything
In the best modern way—the children's eyes
In momentary wonder stare upon
A sixty-year old smiling public man.[6]

Reciting either or both of these poems aloud reveals what is meant by the mystery of the music of a poem. The very sound says what is happening in the poem. In Yeats's poem, the longest line is about the "long schoolroom," thus echoing the feeling of the poet having to walk through that long room. The reader knows from the very sound of the line that the poet is doing more than questioning the children. He is growing old, questioning life and modern methods of doing things. Putting the long word, *questioning*, at the very end of the line emphasizes this mood.

These are more than merely technical matters. The sounds of words, the length of lines, speak to the whole person, especially when recited aloud. They echo the human heart beating to different circumstances, either evoking melancholy, as in Yeat's lines, or confirming the seriousness of plague in the lines by Nashe. Recite aloud the poems you love, and something more happens than if you read them silently. The unconscious overtones of the sounds of the words strengthen their conscious meaning.

9. Write Your Own Canticle

Writing is a way of seeing. It helps you to gather the elements of your world, name them, and order them. If you were to write a Canticle of Praise, what would you praise God for? Of all your experiences, what would you choose?

Such an endeavor is very helpful. Perhaps it may be an unexpected revelation that your prayer has focused mainly on asking God for favors, with little or no attention to the wonderful works of God in the world and in your personal life. Writing a Canticle also helps to focus your attention on concrete, specific things instead of generalities, things that call out to be lifted up to God in praise and thanksgiving. The result is often a profound sense of gratitude and awe for so many gifts of God that have gone unnoticed, or have been taken for granted.

One way of beginning such a Canticle is to name the most important gifts in your life and write a stanza of praise for one of the gifts each day. Then name the things you are most grateful for in nature, and again, write a stanza for each. As you write, there may be some interesting discoveries: your name for God; the order in which you put the gifts, and why; the adjectives you use to describe each gift; how much time you must spend in prayer and reflection before you can begin each stanza; how hard it is to really look closely at each gift.

Since a Canticle's movement is outward, it broadens one's prayer beyond the narrow confines of the kind of self-absorption which can sometimes turn prayer into an exercise of self-analysis rather than an opening up to God. You may also discover that your Canticle shows you a map of your inner and outer world, the unique person you are. What a gift it is to be who you are, and to praise God as only you can! This sense of wholeness comes not from dwelling on yourself, but from dwelling on God and God's gifts that are uniquely yours.

Suggested Poems for Prayer

Brother Antoninus (William Everson)
Canticle to the Water Birds

Craig, David
The Sandaled Foot

Deane, John F.
The Fox-God

Erdrich, Louise
Saint Clare

Graham, Jorie
At the Exhumed Body of Santa Chiara, Assisi

Harjo, Joy
A Map to the Next World

Heaney, Seamus
St. Francis and the Birds

Notes

Chapter 1
Poetry and Prayer

1. Murray Bodo, O.F.M., *Through the Year with Francis of Assisi* (Cincinnati: St. Anthony Messenger Press, 1987), p. 166.

2. Rainier Maria Rilke, *The Selected Poetry of Rainier Maria Rilke* edited and translated by Stephen Mitchell. (New York: Vintage International, 1989), p. 91.

Chapter 2
The Life of St. Francis

1. Thomas of Celano, "The Life of St. Francis," chapter III, par. 6, in *Francis of Assisi: Early Documents*, vol. 1 (New York: New City Press, 1999), pp. 187–188.

2. Cf. Eloi Leclerc, *The Canticle of the Creatures: Symbols of Union* (Chicago: Franciscan Herald Press, 1977).

3. Murray Bodo, O.F.M., *Through the Year with Francis of Assisi*, p. 82.

4. Ibid., p. 133.

5. Thomas of Celano, "Second Life," *St. Francis of Assisi: Writings and Early Biographies: English Omnibus of Sources for the Life of St. Francis* (Chicago: Franciscan Herald Press, 1983), p. 214.

Chapter 3
Francis, the Poet

1. Thomas of Celano, "Second Life," *St. Francis of Assisi: Writings and Early Biographies: English Omnibus of Sources for the Life of St. Francis* (Chicago: Franciscan Herald Press, 1983), p. 467.

2. Murray Bodo, O.F.M., *Through the Year with Francis of Assisi*, pp. 120–121.

3. *The Little Flowers of St. Francis*, author's translation, *Fonti Francescane: Editio Minor* (Padova: Editrici Francescane, 1986), p. 883.

4. Dante, *The Divine Comedy*, vol. III, "Paradise," translated by Mark Musa (New York: Penguin Putnam, Inc., 1986), *Canto XI*, p. 135.

5. Michael Weldon, *Francis of Assisi and Troubadour Song,* dissertation (Berkeley: University of California, 1982), p. 179.

6. Thomas of Celano, "Second Life," *St. Francis of Assisi: Writings and Early Biographies: English Omnibus of Sources for the Life of St. Francis* (Chicago: Franciscan Herald Press, 1983), p. 235.

7. Cf. Adrian House, *Francis of Assisi: A Revolutionary Life* (Mahwah, NJ: Hidden Spring / Paulist Press, 2001), pp. 158–161.

8. St. Bonaventure, "Major Life of St. Francis," in *English Ominibus of Sources,* p. 698.

Chapter 4
The Canticle of St. Francis

1. "Legend of Perugia," *English Omnibus of Sources,* pp. 1020–1021.

2. Gaston Bachelard, *Water and Dreams: An Essay on the Imagination of Matter* (Dallas: The Pegasus Foundation, 1983), p. 93.

Chapter 5
A Meditation on the Canticle

1. Ilia Delio, *Franciscan Studies,* vol. 52, St. Bonaventure (NY: The Franciscan Institute, 1992), p. 10.

2. Murray Bodo, O.F.M., *Through the Year with Francis of Assisi,* p. 58

3. Edward A. Armstrong, *St. Francis: Nature Mystic* (Berkeley: University of California Press, 1973), p. 242.

4. Murray Bodo, O.F.M., *Through the Year with Francis of Assisi,* pp. 167–168.

5. *The Liturgy of the Hours,* Tuesday of Week 33, the Second Reading (New York: Catholic Book Publishing Co., 1976).

6. Murray Bodo, O.F.M., *Francis: The Journey and the Dream* (Cincinnati: St. Anthony Messenger Press, 1988), p. 51.

7. Author's rendering of Thomas of Celano's, "Treatise on the Miracles," *Fonti Francescane: Editio Minor* (Padova: Editrici Francescane, 1986), p. 464.

8. St. Bonaventure, "Major Life of St. Francis," in *English Omnibus of Sources,* p. 698.

9. Murray Bodo, O.F.M., *Through the Year with Francis of Assisi*, pp. 103–104.

10. Author's rendering of Thomas of Celano's, "Treatise on the Miracles," *Fonti Francescane: Editio Minor* (Padova: Editrici Francescane, 1986), II Celano, chapter 11, n. 16–17.

11. *The Little Flowers of St. Francis*, op. cit., p. 15.

12. Thomas of Celano in *English Omnibus of the Sources*, I. Celano, 47, p. 698.

13. Murray Bodo, O.F.M., *Through the Year with Francis of Assisi*, p. 178.

14. Ibid, p. 124.

15. Ibid, p. 185

16. Ibid, p. 186.

Chapter 6
Ways to Read Poetry Prayerfully

1. "Father & Son," from *The Collected Poems* by Stanley Kunitz.

2. Murray Bodo, O.F.M., *Through the Year with Francis of Assisi*, p. 94.

3. Murray Bodo, O.F.M., *Icarus in Assisi* (Assisi: Minerva Press, 2002).

4. Edward Hirsch, *How to Read a Poem and Fall in Love with Poetry*, p. 16.

5. "A Litany in Time of Plague" by Thomas Nasche, as quoted in Edward Hirsch, op. cit., p. 306.

6. "Among Schoolchildren" is reprinted with the permission of Scribner, a Division of Simon & Schuster, Inc., from *The Collected Poems of W.B. Yeats: Volume 1, The Poems, Revised.* Edited by Richard J. Finneran.

Acknowledgments

The quote beginning "And yet it is not enough…" is from *The Selected Poetry of Rainer Maria Rilke* by Rainer Maria Rilke, translated by Stephen Mitchell, copyright © 1982 by Stephen Mitchell. Used by permission of Random House, Inc.

The English translation of a discourse by St. Andrew of Crete (p. 83) from *The Liturgy of the Hours* © 1974, International Committee on English in the Liturgy, Inc. All rights reserved.

"Father & Son," from *The Collected Poems* by Stanley Kunitz. Copyright © 2000 by Stanley Kunitz. Used by permission of W. W. Norton & Company, Inc.

Excerpt from *How to Read a Poem and Fall in Love with Poetry*, copyright © 1999 by Edward Hirsch, reprinted by permission of Harcourt, Inc.

Murray Bodo is a Franciscan priest and a member of the Franciscan Academy. The author of fifteen books, including the best-selling *Francis: The Journey and the Dream*, his poems, stories, and articles have been published in magazines and literary journals. Fr. Murray resides in Cincinnati, Ohio, and spends his summers in Assisi, as a staff member of "Franciscan Pilgrimage Programs."

auline
BOOKS & MEDIA

The Daughters of St. Paul operate book and media centers at the following addresses. Visit, call or write the one nearest you today, or find us on the World Wide Web, www.pauline.org

CALIFORNIA
3908 Sepulveda Blvd, Culver City, CA
  90230   310-397-8676
5945 Balboa Avenue, San Diego, CA
  92111   858-565-9181
46 Geary Street, San Francisco, CA
  94108   415-781-5180

FLORIDA
145 S.W. 107th Avenue, Miami, FL
  33174   305-559-6715

HAWAII
1143 Bishop Street, Honolulu, HI
  96813   808-521-2731
Neighbor Islands call: 800-259-8463

ILLINOIS
172 North Michigan Avenue,
  Chicago, IL 60601
  312-346-4228

LOUISIANA
4403 Veterans Blvd, Metairie, LA
  70006   504-887-7631

MASSACHUSETTS
885 Providence Hwy,
  Dedham, MA 02026
  781-326-5385

MISSOURI
9804 Watson Road,
  St. Louis, MO 63126
  314-965-3512

NEW JERSEY
561 U.S. Route 1, Wick Plaza,
  Edison, NJ 08817
  732-572-1200

NEW YORK
150 East 52nd Street, New York, NY
  10022   212-754-1110
78 Fort Place, Staten Island, NY
  10301   718-447-5071

PENNSYLVANIA
9171-A Roosevelt Blvd, Philadelphia,
  PA 19114   215-676-9494

SOUTH CAROLINA
243 King Street, Charleston, SC
  29401   843-577-0175

TENNESSEE
4811 Poplar Avenue, Memphis, TN
  38117   901-761-2987

TEXAS
114 Main Plaza, San Antonio, TX
  78205   210-224-8101

VIRGINIA
1025 King Street, Alexandria, VA
  22314   703-549-3806

CANADA
3022 Dufferin Street, Toronto, Ontario,
  Canada M6B 3T5   416-781-9131
1155 Yonge Street, Toronto, Ontario,
  Canada M4T 1W2   416-934-3440

¡También somos su fuente para libros, videos y música en español!